MW01631110

one step ahead *Cookbook*

photography by Martin Brigdale

MARY BERRY
one step ahead *Cookbook*

Over 100 delicious recipes made easy

Quadrille
PUBLISHING

This book is dedicated with a big thank-you to Lucy Young, who has been working with me now for some seventeen years.

This edition first published in 2010 by **Quadrille Publishing Limited,**
Alhambra House, 27–31 Charing Cross Road, London WC2H OLS

Editorial Director: **Jane O'Shea**
Creative Director: **Helen Lewis**
Editor and Project Manager: **Lewis Esson**
Art Director: **Mary Evans**
Photography: **Martin Brigdale**
Styling: **Helen Trent**
Food Styling: **Annie Rigg**
Production: **Vincent Smith, Ruth Deary**

Cataloguing in Publication Data: a catalogue record for this book is available from the British Library

ISBN 978 184400 906 0

Printed and bound in China

My cooking is very much about really good food, using quality ingredients to achieve wonderful results.

We all have busy lives, and in my case the family is growing, so we enjoy informal entertaining, often round the kitchen table, and as a result I really do regularly get 'One Step Ahead' with my cooking. So, when Quadrille asked me to put pen to paper 18 months ago, I was delighted. This book was right up my street.

I am, anyway, generally a fairly organised person and I find this invaluable when having friends or family for supper. However, I only prepare ahead when the dish is just as good cooked in advance as it is when served immediately. You'll see that in each recipe I give a holding point to which the recipe can be taken and tell you how long this can be. This information will give you confidence and the knowledge that your food is going to be served on time as well as be delicious. Often the whole dish can be made ahead, but sometimes it may just be the sauce. Cooking 'One Step Ahead' – earlier in the day or on the day before – means you can relax and enjoy time with your friends when they arrive.

In each recipe I also mention whether or not a dish can be frozen. If it can, always make sure your dish is completely cold and well wrapped before freezing, and remember, the quality of the dish you are freezing will be the same as the quality of the dish you are defrosting! If time allows, I always prefer to defrost the dishes I have frozen in the fridge.

It is important to use the freshest of ingredients and the best quality you can afford – this is the secret to good cooking. In the recipes in this book, you will see that I have often made use of basic store-cupboard ingredients. The advantage of this is that you are always prepared and have the staples to hand. However, I don't use too many different such ingredients. I like to stick to the same spices that I use fairly often and keep to basics like *mango chutney, Worcestershire sauce, dark soy sauce, hoisin sauce and fish sauce, so you won't end up having a cupboard full of ingredients that you may only use for one recipe. Any opened jars or bottles should be kept in the fridge, and spices should be kept in the dark to prevent them from discolouring and losing their flavour. For example, in some recipes I have cheated a bit and used ready-made pesto – this is to make life easier and preparation quicker. Also, some of the ready-made ingredients like this you can buy now are of very good quality indeed.*

As an aside, I am thrilled there are so many photographs in this book. The photography is stunning and on some recipes there are also step-by-step pictures to guide you along the way, so the illustrations are as useful as they are enticing.

Cooking should be a pleasure – a joy for you to do and a delight for your guests to enjoy. I hope that this book will make life easier for you in the kitchen and give you peace of mind... and that you always enjoy being 'One Step Ahead'.

Mary Berry

party *nibbles*

Soft-poached quails' eggs should be runny in the middle. Do warn your guests about this before eating, so that they don't get drips down their posh clothes! I learnt how to poach quails' eggs when I was at The Raymond Blanc Cookery School at Le Manoir Aux Quat' Saisons. It was a great tip from the head tutor. Most good supermarkets sell long thin baguettes that will cut into about 50 slices to make these crostini bases.

courgette and QUAILS' egg tapas

MAKES 24

1/2 long thin baguette
a little butter, softened
olive oil for frying
2 small courgettes, chopped into very small dice
2 tablespoons pesto
1 tablespoon white wine vinegar
24 quails' eggs

Line a baking tray with non-stick parchment paper.

Cut the baguette half into 24 slices about 5mm (1/4 inch) thick and spread one side of each with a little butter. Arrange, buttered side down, on the prepared tray.

Heat the oil in a frying pan and fry the courgette dice for about 3 minutes until soft and light golden brown. Stir in the pesto and season with salt and pepper. Set aside to cool.

When cool, spoon the courgette mixture on to the pieces of bread.

To poach the quails' eggs, bring a large shallow pan of water with the vinegar in it up to the boil. Crack 12 of the eggs into a small bowl. Whisk the boiling water, and then quickly pour in the eggs. Bring the water back up to the boil, then, using a draining spoon, scoop out the eggs and put them into a bowl of cold water. Trim any extra untidy white from the eggs. Repeat this process with the remaining quails' eggs using the same water.

● ***The eggs can be poached a day ahead, then reheated when needed. The bread slices can be topped with the courgettes up to 8 hours ahead. Neither are suitable for freezing.***

When ready to cook, preheat the oven to 220°C/200°C fan/gas 7 and cook the topped bread slices in the oven for about 8 minutes until hot.

While they are in the oven, fill a bowl with hot water from the tap and carefully drop in the eggs for about 5 minutes to reheat them, then put one on each piece of bread when it comes out of the oven. You'll need to make a slight indentation in the courgettes ready to take the egg. Season lightly.

AGA COOKING Bake the tapas on the floor of the roasting oven for about 8 minutes.

Buy the type of hard goats' cheese that comes in a roll with a white crusty rind on it, as this will keep its shape when sliced and baked, without running off the piece of baguette. Sun-blushed tomatoes are sometimes called sun-ripened tomatoes and can be found at the deli counter in good supermarkets.

goats' cheese, OLIVE and tomato TAPAS

MAKES 24

1/2 long thin baguette
a little butter, softened
a little sun-dried tomato paste
2 (120g) hard goats' cheeses (see above), chilled
12 sun-blushed tomatoes, halved
24 small black pitted olives

Cut the baguette into 24 slices about 5mm (1/4 inch) thick and spread one side of each with butter. Arrange buttered side down on a baking sheet lined with non-stick paper. Spread the top of the slices with a little sun-dried tomato paste.

Cut the cheese into 24 slices, keeping the rind on. Put one slice of cheese on each piece of bread, then top with half a sun-blushed tomato and one olive.

● ***Make up to 12 hours ahead of cooking. Not suitable for freezing.***

Bake in an oven preheated to 220°C/200°C fan/gas 7 until golden brown, for about 8 minutes.

AGA COOKING Slide the baking sheet on to the floor of the roasting oven for about 7 minutes, until the crostini are golden brown underneath.

If you have any soft, spreadable cheese, such as Brie, Camembert or Vignotte, left from the cheeseboard, you could use it instead of Boursin. The red pepper for these can be fresh, canned or Peppadew peppers from a jar *(see page 71)**.*

Boursin, red pepper and onion crostini

MAKES 24

1/2 long thin baguette
a little butter, softened
1 tablespoon olive oil
1 small onion, finely chopped
1 red pepper, deseeded and chopped into 1cm (1/2 inch) dice
150g Boursin cheese

Cut the baguette into 24 slices about 5mm (1/4 inch) thick and spread one side of each with a little butter. Arrange the slices buttered side down on a baking sheet lined with non-stick paper.

Heat the oil in a frying pan, add the onion and fry it for about 5 minutes, or until it is starting to soften. Then add the pepper and fry over a high heat for another 5 minutes until the pepper and onion are golden brown. Allow to cool and then season to taste.

Spread the Boursin cheese on the tops of the pieces of bread, then spoon the pepper mixture on top of the cheese.

● ***Make up to 12 hours ahead of cooking. These are not suitable for freezing.***

Bake in an oven preheated to 220°C/200°C fan/gas 7 for about 8 minutes, until golden brown and the bases are crisp.

AGA COOKING Slide the baking sheet on to the floor of the roasting oven for about 8 minutes until the slices are golden brown underneath.

These are so quick to make because they use ready-rolled puff pastry. I prefer the colour of green pesto for this recipe, but if you only have red pesto in your cupboard this will be just as good.

fast PESTO parmesan CHEESE straws

MAKES 24

1 (375g) packet of ready-rolled puff pastry
2 good tablespoons green pesto
75g (3 oz) Parmesan cheese, grated
1 egg, beaten

Lay the pastry out on a floured work surface and re-roll to a large rectangle about 17 x 40cm, so the pastry is paper-thin. Cut the pastry in half lengthways to make 2 rectangular pieces.

Spread pesto on one side of one of the pieces. Sprinkle 50g (2 oz) of the Parmesan cheese over the other piece. Place the pesto piece on top of the Parmesan piece so that the Parmesan and pesto are in contact, press together gently and chill for at least 30 minutes.

Preheat the oven to 200°C/180°C fan/gas 6. Trim the edges of the pastry, brush with beaten egg and sprinkle with the remaining cheese. Cut into 2cm (1 inch) wide strips.

Arrange on non-stick paper on a baking sheet and bake in the preheated oven for about 12-15 minutes, until golden brown and crisp.

● ***These can be made up to a week ahead, and kept in the fridge in a sealed box. Refresh in a cool oven just to warm through. They also freeze well, layered in a box with kitchen paper.***

AGA COOKING Bake on the grid shelf on the floor of the roasting oven for about 15 minutes until golden brown and crisp. If still pale underneath, you may need to remove the grid shelf and bake on the floor of the oven for the last 5 minutes.

These are delicious and will be loved by all – perfect to serve with drinks before a meal or to accompany soup.

PARMESAN and tomato biscuits

MAKES about 50

100g (4oz) flour
100g (4oz) butter
50g (2oz) mature Cheddar cheese, grated
50g (2oz) Parmesan cheese, grated
1 good tablespoon sun-dried tomato paste

Measure all the ingredients into a food processor and whiz until smooth. Remove from the processor and shape into a ball. Cover with cling film and chill for at least 30 minutes.

Preheat the oven to 180°C/160C° fan/gas 4 and line a baking sheet with baking parchment.

Flour a work surface and roll the dough out thinly. Using a 3cm ($1\frac{1}{2}$ inch) pastry cutter, cut out about 50 rounds.

Arrange these on the prepared baking sheet and bake in the preheated oven for about 6–7 minutes, until pale golden brown (slightly darker than shortbread) and cooked through.

● ***The cooked biscuits can be made up to 3 days ahead and kept in the fridge. They also freeze well. Refresh in a moderate oven for a couple of minutes before serving, warm or cold.***

AGA COOKING Bake on the grid shelf on the floor of the roasting oven for about 6 minutes and watch very carefully.

I prefer to make my own pancakes as I can then make them very thin – bought ones are usually a little thick. You can use full- or half-fat cream cheese, as you prefer.

smoked SALMON and dill canapé pancakes

MAKES about 60 small canapés

FOR THE BATTER

100g (4oz) plain flour
1 egg
100ml (4fl oz) milk
a little sunflower oil for frying

FOR THE FILLING

200g tub of cream cheese
400g (14oz) smoked salmon slices
4 tablespoons chopped fresh dill

First make the pancake batter: measure the flour into a bowl, add the egg and one-third of the milk, then whisk well until smooth. Stir in the rest of the milk.

Heat a small non-stick frying pan (about 20cm/8 inches), add a little oil just to cover the base and heat. Pour in just enough pancake mixture to line the base of the pan. Cook until brown underneath, flip over and cook the other side. Cook more pancakes in the same way using the rest of the batter.

Once the pancakes are cold, spread a thin layer of cream cheese over one side of each pancake and season with black pepper. Lay a layer of smoked salmon over the top of the cream cheese and sprinkle over some chopped fresh dill.

Roll the pancakes into a tight cigar shape. Wrap in cling film and chill.

● *The unfilled pancakes can be made up to 24 hours ahead and kept, covered, in the fridge. The wrapped filled and rolled pancakes can be kept in the fridge for up to 8 hours.*

Cut each pancake across at an angle into 10 very thin slices, arrange on a plate and serve as a canapé.

AGA COOKING Cook the first side of the pancake in a pan on the boiling plate for a minute, then continue to cook the other side on the simmering plate.

It is always nice to have a hot canapé with drinks. This one is very quick and easy to do, as well as looking especially impressive. Don't worry if you don't have Chinese spoons, any teaspoon will do. They can even be served on cocktail sticks.

hot PRAWNS on chinese spoons

pictured on page 20

MAKES 20

20 raw king prawns, peeled
½ cucumber, peeled, halved lengthways, deseeded and very thinly sliced into thin strips
small bunch of coriander leaves

FOR THE MARINADE

2cm (1 inch) piece of fresh ginger, peeled and finely grated
finely grated zest and juice of ½ lime
1 tablespoon sweet chilli sauce
1 tablespoon soy sauce

Mix the marinade ingredients together in a bowl.

Add the prawns with some seasoning and toss to coat the prawns. Cover with cling film and chill for 30 minutes.

● ***Marinate up to an hour ahead but no longer. These are not suitable for freezing.***

Remove the prawns from the marinade and cook in a hot non-stick frying pan over a high heat for 30 seconds on each side, until cooked and pink.

Put one prawn on each spoon, then pour the marinade into the same pan and reduce over a high heat for a few minutes until the marinade has thickened and darkened in colour. Spoon this over the hot prawns.

Garnish each spoon with fine strips of cucumber and a coriander leaf.

AGA COOKING Slide the prawns on to the floor of the roasting oven for about 7 minutes until just cooked and pink.

This is my favourite special nibble to go with drinks. Most good supermarkets sell long thin baguettes that will slice into about 50 slices to make the bases for these crostini. You would think that this Marie Rose sauce (the kind you use for prawn cocktail) mixture would curdle on heating, but it doesn't and it is remarkably easy to make.

prawn COCKTAIL crostini

pictured on page 21

MAKES 24

1/2 long thin baguette
a little butter, softened
4 tablespoons light mayonnaise
2 tablespoons tomato ketchup
dash of Worcestershire sauce
dash of lemon juice
200g (7oz) shelled cooked North Atlantic prawns
paprika

Cut the baguette into 24 slices about 5mm (1/4 inch) thick and spread one side of each with a little butter. Arrange buttered side down on a baking sheet lined with non-stick paper or greaseproof paper.

In a bowl, mix together the mayonnaise, ketchup, Worcestershire sauce and lemon juice. Add the really well drained prawns, with some seasoning and spoon the mixture on top of the pieces of bread, so that each one has about 2–3 prawns each. Sprinkle with paprika.

● ***Make up to 12 hours ahead and keep covered in the fridge. Sprinkle with the paprika just before cooking. Not suitable for freezing.***

Cook in the oven preheated to 220°C/200°C fan/gas 7 for about 8 minutes until golden brown.

AGA COOKING Slide the crostini on to the floor of the roasting oven for about 8 minutes or until golden brown underneath and tinged brown on top.

This is a fresher, more up-to-date version of the traditional savoury dish served at the end of meals, devils-on-horseback – prunes wrapped in bacon.

APRICOTS wrapped in bacon

MAKES 20

10 very thin slices of smoked streaky bacon
10 soft dried apricots

Cut each slice of bacon across in half widthways. Cut each apricot into two and wrap each piece tightly with a piece of bacon.

● ***They can be made up to this stage and kept in the fridge up to 48 hours ahead of cooking. They also freeze well uncooked.***

Bake in an oven preheated to 220°C/200°C fan/gas 7 for about 10 minutes, until the bacon is crisp.

Variations

For a change, replace the apricots with water chestnuts from a can. Drain and cut each chestnut in half. Wrap in bacon, pour over a little honey and cook as above.

AGA COOKING Bake on the top set of runners in the roasting oven for about 8–10 minutes.

This makes a very good variation on the basic recipe for all those who enjoy hummus. Let it come to room temperature for 15 minutes before serving to get the full flavour.

sun-dried tomato and butter bean hummus

SERVES 6

1 large (410g) tin of butter beans, drained and rinsed
1 large garlic clove, sliced in half
1 small bunch of flat-leaf parsley
175g (6 oz) sun-dried tomatoes in oil
150g (5 oz) low-fat Greek-style yoghurt
juice of 1 lemon
warmed pitta bread, to serve

Put the butter beans, garlic and parsley into a food processor and whiz until the ingredients are chopped. Add the sun-dried tomatoes and 4 tablespoons of their oil together with the yoghurt and lemon juice. Whiz again until smooth and then season to taste.

● ***The dip will keep up to 3 days in the fridge. It is not suitable for freezing.***

Serve with warmed pitta bread.

first *courses*

This is not unlike the parsnip curry soup invented by Jane Grigson many moons ago. Now that English celeriac is plentiful in late summer and over the winter, it is an interesting variation. Peel the celeriac with a small sharp knife – because it is so knobbly it will be impossible to do with a vegetable peeler. Celeriac is always cheaper in farm shops, straight from the ground with no fancy wrapping.

CELERIAC soup with a hint of curry

SERVES 6

75g (3 oz) butter
2 large onions, chopped
3 garlic cloves, crushed
40g (1½ oz) flour
1 level tablespoon curry powder
1.8 litre (3 pints) vegetable or chicken stock
675g (1½ lb) celeriac, peeled and cut into 2cm (1 inch) cubes
150ml (¼ pint) single cream
chive stalks, snipped

Melt the butter in a deep saucepan. Add the onions and fry them over high heat for about 5–10 minutes. Add the garlic, then sprinkle in the flour and curry powder. Stir in the stock and bring to the boil.

Add the celeriac, cover and simmer for about 20–30 minutes until tender.

Strain the soup, put the vegetables into a food processor and whiz until completely smooth. Return the liquid and the puréed vegetables to the pan. Bring to the boil. Season with salt and pepper, and stir in half the cream.

● *The soup can be made up to 2 days ahead. It also freezes well.*

Pour the soup into bowls, swirl a little of the remaining cream on top and sprinkle with the chives.

AGA COOKING Cook on the boiling plate up to the boiling of the stock. Add the celeriac, bring to boil, cover and transfer to the simmering oven for about 30–35 minutes until tender. Continue as above.

This soup is smooth but you can keep some of the pepper back before whizzing if you would prefer a little texture. The colour of the soup is stunning and it is also very healthy, as there is no fat or flour, just pure vegetables. Ensure that the sweet potato and pepper pieces are cut the same size, so they will then take the same time to cook.

red pepper and SWEET POTATO soup

SERVES 6

675g ($1^1/_2$ lb) sweet potato, peeled
2 red peppers, deseeded and cut into large chunks
1 large onion, chopped
1.5 litres ($2^1/_2$ pints) chicken or vegetable stock

Cut the sweet potatoes into even-sized pieces about 5cm (2 inches).

Tip them into a large deep saucepan, add the remaining ingredients and bring to the boil over a high heat. Boil for a few minutes, season to taste, cover, lower the heat and simmer for about 20 minutes, or until the potatoes are tender.

Strain the soup and put the vegetables into a food processor, then whiz until smooth. Return the liquid and the puréed vegetables to the pan and bring to the boil, season with salt and pepper and serve hot.

● ***The soup can be made completely up to 2 days ahead and reheated to serve. When reheating, stir well so that the thickest purée doesn't sink to the bottom of the pan. The soup freezes well.***

AGA COOKING Bring to the boil on the boiling plate, cover and transfer to the simmering oven for about an hour, until tender.

Serve this simple soup with a main course that isn't spicy, so it complements the soup. Home-cooked beetroot is far better than bought - and cheaper. Cut off the leaves about 4cm (2 inches) above the root and don't trim the root, or the colour bleeds. Simmer in water until tender – about an hour, depending on size. Allow to cool in their skins.

thai BEETROOT soup

SERVES 4-6

1 tablespoon oil
1 large onion, finely chopped
500g (1 lb) cooked beetroot, peeled and roughly chopped
1½ teaspoons red Thai curry paste
1 (400 ml) can of coconut milk
300 ml (½ pint) chicken stock
juice of ½ lime
2 tablespoons chopped parsley

Heat the oil in a large saucepan over a high heat. Add the onion, lower the heat, cover and cook for about 10 minutes to soften the onion.

Add two-thirds of the beetroot to the onions, stir in the Thai paste and fry for couple of minutes over high heat. Stir in the coconut milk and stock, season with salt and pepper to taste, bring to the boil, cover and simmer over a low heat for about 5 minutes.

Whiz in a food processor until smooth. Pour back into the pan, add the remaining beetroot and lime juice and adjust the seasoning, if necessary.

● ***This soup can be made up to 24 hours ahead and kept in the fridge. It is not suitable for freezing.***

Sprinkle with parsley and serve hot.

AGA COOKING Soften the onion on the boiling plate for a few minutes, cover and transfer to the simmering oven for about 15 minutes.

This was a great favourite with everyone on our last family holiday – it is so easy to make and is a meal in itself with crusty bread. Choose any fish that you like – it is best to use white fish rather than salmon, herring or mackerel.

TOMATO bouillabaisse

SERVES 6

- 1 tablespoon oil
- 3 shallots, finely chopped
- 2 celery stalks, finely chopped
- 3 garlic cloves, crushed
- 2 (400g) cans of chopped tomatoes
- 900ml ($1^1/_2$ pints) fish or vegetable stock
- 2 tablespoons tomato paste
- dash of sugar
- 650g (1lb 5oz) mixed skinned and boned white fish, such as monkfish, haddock or cod, cut into 2cm (1inch) cubes
- 100g (4oz) shelled cooked North Atlantic prawns
- 2 tablespoons chopped fresh parsley

Heat the oil in a large saucepan, add the shallots and celery, and fry for 2 minutes until softened.

Add the garlic, tomatoes with their liquid, stock and tomato paste. Stir and bring to the boil. Add the sugar and salt and pepper to taste. Cover and simmer over a low heat for about 15 minutes, until the shallots are tender.

● *If making ahead, at this stage cover and chill for up to 2 days. Then reheat and add the fish and prawns. This is not suitable for freezing.*

Remove the lid, add the fish and prawns, bring back to the boil and simmer for about 3 minutes, until the fish is just cooked.

Sprinkle in the parsley and serve hot.

AGA COOKING Make on the boiling plate before adding the fish, then cover and transfer to simmering oven for about 15 minutes, until the shallots are tender. Continue on the simmering plate.

This mousse served with an avocado and cherry tomato salsa make a very smart first course. If you would prefer to make one big mousse, turn the mixture into an 800ml ring mould or soufflé dish.

AVOCADO and cucumber mousse

with cherry tomato salsa

SERVES 8

vegetable oil, for greasing
1 large cucumber
15g packet of gelatine
1 ripe avocado, stoned, peeled and roughly chopped
200g (7 oz) low-fat cream cheese
200g (7 oz) half-fat crème fraîche
6 good tablespoons light mayonnaise
juice of 1/2 lemon
150ml (1/4 pint) warm chicken stock
2 tablespoons chopped dill

FOR THE AVOCADO AND CHERRY TOMATO SALSA

1 avocado, stoned, peeled and very finely diced
3 tablespoons lemon juice
4 tablespoons olive oil
175g (6 oz) cherry tomatoes, deseeded and thinly sliced
2 tablespoons chopped dill

Lightly grease the sides of eight size-1 (150 ml) ramekins with a little oil.

Peel the cucumber, cut it in half lengthways and remove the seeds with a teaspoon. Chop into very small dice. Put the cucumber in a sieve and sprinkle over a teaspoon of salt. Leave for about 1 hour until some liquid has drained from the cucumber, then rinse in cold water and pat dry.

Measure 3 tablespoons of cold water into a small bowl. Sprinkle over the gelatine and leave to sponge for about 10 minutes. Once sponged, stand the bowl in a pan containing a little boiling water to dissolve the gelatine.

Put the avocado, cream cheese, crème fraîche, mayonnaise and lemon juice into a food processor and whiz until smooth. Pour the gelatine into the warm chicken stock, mix together, then pour into the food processor while the motor is running and continue to run until blended. Remove the blade then stir in the diced cucumber and dill, and season.

Pour the mixture into the ramekins. Cover with cling film and chill in the fridge for at least 6 hours, until firm.

● ***The mousses can be made up to 48 hours ahead. They are not suitable for freezing.***

Mix all the salsa ingredients together in a bowl and season. Run a thin small palette knife around the edges of the ramekins, then tip the mousses upside down on a plate and shake to release them from the ramekins. Spoon the salsa alongside the mousse.

AGA COOKING Cook on the top set of runners in the roasting oven for about 8 minutes.

The contrast of a double layer of fish in two colours is exciting to cut through and the flavours are delicate. If you have an abundance of dill, you might like to add it to the sauce instead of the spinach.

double FISH mousselines

SERVES 8

350g (12oz) halibut, skinned and cut into cubes
4 egg whites
2 tablespoons lemon juice
freshly grated nutmeg
300ml (1/2 pint) double cream
1 tablespoon chopped dill
350g (12oz) salmon fillet, skinned and cut into cubes
1/2 teaspoon paprika
butter, for the ramekins

FOR THE SAUCE

150ml (1/4 pint) white wine
300ml (1/2 pint) double cream
50g (2oz) spinach, finely chopped
2 tablespoons lemon juice
chopped parsley

First make the mousselines: put the halibut into a food processor, add half the egg whites together with 1 tablespoon lemon juice, a little grated nutmeg and some seasoning. Whiz together until very smooth then, with the motor running, pour in half the double cream. Spoon into a small bowl and stir in the dill.

Put the salmon in the unwashed processor, and add remaining egg whites, 1 tablespoon of lemon juice, the paprika and some seasoning. Whiz until smooth, then add the remaining cream, whizzing until it is all blended together.

Line the bases of 8 small ramekins with a disc of Bakewell paper and butter the sides. Spoon the halibut mixture into the bases and level the top. Spoon the salmon mixture on top of the halibut and level. Make sure you wipe any mix off the rims of the ramekins.

● ***You can make these ready for the oven up to 12 hours ahead and make the sauce without the spinach. Cook the mousselines when needed and reheat the sauce, thinning it down with a little water if necessary, adding the spinach at the last moment. This is not suitable for freezing.***

Preheat the oven to 200°C/180°C fan/gas 6. Arrange the ramekins in a large roasting tin and fill with boiling water to come halfway up the sides of the ramekins. Cover the tin with foil and carefully slide it into the preheated oven for about 10–12 minutes. Take out of the oven and leave to rest, covered with the foil, for another 10–12 minutes.

Meanwhile, make the sauce: pour the wine into a large saucepan and boil to reduce by half. Add the cream and spinach, and season well. Bring to the boil again, then add the lemon juice.

Turn the mousselines out on a plate, remove the paper and spoon over a little sauce. Serve sprinkled with parsley.

AGA COOKING Slide the tin on the grid shelf on the floor of the roasting oven for 10–12 minutes, turning the tin around halfway through the cooking time. Remove from the oven and leave to rest, covered, for 10–12 minutes.

These are perfect for a light supper as well as a starter. Smoked mackerel usually comes in vacuum packs and just requires the removal of the skin, which slips off easily.

hot-smoked MACKEREL and tomato tian

SERVES 6

4 large tomatoes, skinned and each one sliced into 3
25g (1 oz) butter
175g (6 oz) button chestnut mushrooms, sliced
250g (9 oz) smoked mackerel fillets, skinned
150ml (1/4 pint) double cream
1 teaspoon grainy mustard
juice of 1/2 lemon
1 tablespoon chopped parsley

You will need 6 metal cooking rings with a diameter of 7cm (2 3/4 inches). Sit these on a sheet of non-stick paper on a baking sheet. Put a slice of tomato in the base of each ring.

Heat a frying pan and add the butter. Fry the mushrooms and season them. Divide them among the rings, on top of the tomato slices.

Flake the mackerel fillets into large pieces and place on top of the mushrooms, sprinkle with black pepper. Arrange the remaining tomato slices on top of the mackerel.

● ***You can prepare to this point up to 12 hours ahead and keep the uncooked tians in the fridge, then cook when needed for a few minutes longer, as they will be straight out of the fridge. They are not suitable for freezing.***

Bake in an oven preheated to 200°C/180°Cfan/gas 6 for about 10 minutes until hot.

Meanwhile, heat the double cream in a small pan and bring to the boil. Stir in the mustard, lemon juice and seasoning.

Using a fish slice, transfer each tian to a plate. Pour the mustard cream sauce around the tians and sprinkle with the parsley.

AGA COOKING Cook on the top set of runners in the roasting oven for about 8 minutes.

We also make this wonderful and impressive pâté in a triangular tin and in a 450g (1lb) loaf tin. Just dampen the sides of the tin and then line it with cling film. Lay smoked salmon slices along the base and sides so a little is hanging over the edge, then continue as opposite, fill with the prawn mixture and level the top. Fold the overhanging smoked salmon over the top of the pâté to cover, using more smoked salmon if necessary. Press down firmly and chill overnight.

Freezing these for about 30 minutes before serving will make cutting easier. If you have a guest who doesn't eat prawns, take a portion of pâté out of the processor before adding the prawns and fill one ramekin with this. Serve toast or bread with the pâté, but there is no need for butter as it is rich enough. For a less rich and less expensive version, simply line only the base of the ramekins with a disc of smoked salmon.

prawn and smoked SALMON pâté

SERVES 10

- 300g (10oz) smoked salmon slices
- 170g packet of smoked salmon trimmings
- 50g (2oz) butter, softened
- 250g (9oz) full-fat cream cheese
- juice of 1/2 lemon, plus pieces of lemon slice, to serve
- black pepper
- 200g (7oz) shelled cooked North Atlantic prawns
- small bunch of dill, finely chopped
- dressed rocket, to serve

Make the pâté in 10 size-1 (150ml) ramekins. Line the base and sides of each ramekin with cling film, then line the base and sides again with smoked salmon, trim away any excess smoked salmon around the rim.

Put the smoked salmon trimmings and butter into the processor, whiz until well mixed but still very chunky. Add the cream cheese, lemon juice and pepper and whiz again.

Drain the prawns really well on kitchen paper and chop each into 2 or 3 pieces, about the size of peas. Remove the blade from the processor and stir in the prawns and dill.

Spoon into the salmon-lined ramekins and level the top. Fold any overhanging cling film over the top and transfer to the fridge.

● *This can be made a day ahead and kept in the fridge. It also freezes well for up to a month.*

To serve, tip the ramekins upside down on individual plates, remove the cling film and serve garnished with dressed rocket and little lemon points.

If preparing this very popular hot first course ahead, it is best to cook it in the oven rather than under the grill.

garlic mushrooms with BRIE and spinach

SERVES 6

50g (2oz) butter
6 medium field mushrooms, stalks removed
225g (8oz) baby spinach
2 garlic cloves, crushed
2 large beef tomatoes, each sliced into 3 rounds
175g (6oz) ripe Brie, lightly frozen
paprika

If serving immediately, preheat the grill to medium.

Melt half of the butter in a large frying pan. Cook the mushrooms on both sides until they are starting to soften, about 3–4 minutes. Transfer to a baking tray that will fit under the grill. Melt the remaining butter in the pan and fry the spinach until wilted, then add the garlic and some seasoning. Spoon the spinach mixture on top of the mushrooms.

Fry the tomato slices in the pan for a few seconds, then put them on top of the spinach.

Using a potato peeler, shave thin pieces of the Brie over the top of the tomatoes and then sprinkle with a little paprika.

● ***These can be made, covered in cling film and kept in the fridge for up to 12 hours. They are not suitable for freezing.***

If serving immediately, slide the mushrooms under the grill for about 5 minutes, until the mushrooms are hot and the cheese has melted and is golden.

If serving later, preheat the oven to 220°C/200°C fan/gas 6 for about 7–10 minutes until hot and the cheese has melted.

AGA COOKING Bake on top set of runners in the roasting oven for about 8–10 minutes.

This can be served on individual plates as a starter or on a platter to pass round. For the full effect, it is important to use orange-fleshed melon. Try to ensure that the figs are not over-ripe, as they will become mushy when fried. If they are very large, they can be sliced rather than quartered.

parma ham, MELON and warm FIG salad

pictured on page 42

SERVES 8

1/2 just-ripe Cantaloupe melon
3 tablespoons balsamic vinegar
3 tablespoons extra-virgin olive oil
1 (85g) packet of rocket
8 thin slices of Parma ham
8 just-ripe figs, sliced in half through the stem

Remove the seeds from the melon half. Slice it in half, then cut each in half again to give 4 wedges. Remove the peel, then cut ribbons from the melon flesh, using a mandolin grater or a potato peeler (I find it best to do this along the side of the melon wedge). If you find ribbons difficult to cut, just cut the melon in thin slices. Set aside.

Mix the balsamic vinegar and oil together in a bowl and season with salt and pepper.

Arrange the rocket on 8 side plates and arrange the melon and Parma ham over the rocket.

● *The individual plates can be arranged with the rocket, ham and melon, covered in cling film and kept in the fridge for up to 3 hours. The dressing can be made and kept in the bowl. The figs can be fried and dressed just before serving.*

Brush the cut side of the figs with a little oil. Heat a ridged frying pan over high heat and fry the figs, cut side down, for 2 minutes until tinged brown and warm. Arrange two halves on each plate, pour over the dressing and serve at once.

These individual pastry-lined tarts have a bacon, tomato and Taleggio cheese filling. Taleggio is a soft cows'-milk cheese from Northern Italy with a pale orange rind and a distinctive mild but full flavour.

crispy BACON and TALEGGIO tartlets

SERVES 8 (one tartlet each)

FOR THE PASTRY

175g (6oz) plain flour plus more for dusting
75g (3oz) butter
2 tablespoons sun-dried tomato paste
1 egg

FOR THE FILLING

200g (7oz) smoked bacon lardons
75g (3oz) sun-dried tomatoes, snipped into small pieces
200g (7oz) Taleggio cheese, cut into small cubes
2 tablespoons chopped basil
2 eggs, beaten
225ml (8floz) double cream

dressed salad, to serve

Preheat the oven to 200°C/180°C fan/gas 4 and preheat a large heavy baking sheet to very hot.

First make the pastry, measure the flour and butter into a food processor and whiz until resembling breadcrumbs. Add the tomato paste and the egg, and whiz again until it forms a dough.

On a lightly floured surface, roll the dough out thinly and use to line two 4-hole Yorkshire pudding tins.

Heat a dry non-stick frying pan over a high heat. Add the bacon lardons and fry until crisp. Spoon equally between the tartlets.

Divide the tomatoes, cubes of cheese and basil between the tartlets on top of the bacon. Whisk together the eggs and cream, season with salt and pepper and pour into tart cases.

Bake on the now very hot baking sheet for about 15–20 minutes, until golden brown and set.

● ***These tartlets can be made and baked a day ahead and reheated in a hot oven for about 8 minutes. They also freeze well cooked.***

Serve warm with a dressed salad.

AGA COOKING Slide on to the grid shelf on the floor of the roasting oven for about 15 minutes until the pastry is golden brown and the filling is set. Slide directly on the floor of the roasting oven for the last 5 minutes to crisp up the pastry underneath

These make a good first course or light lunch. It's always useful to have a few tartlet tins lined with this pastry in the freezer ready to fill if guests arrive unexpectedly. The pastry must be rolled out thinly so that the result is crisp and light. You can use 225g (8oz) shelled prawns instead of the crab.

thai CRAB tartlets

SERVES 8

FOR THE CHEESE PASTRY

175g (6oz) plain flour
1 teaspoon English mustard powder
75g (3oz) butter, cut into small pieces
50g (2oz) Parmesan cheese, grated
1 egg, beaten

FOR THE FILLING

225ml (8fl oz) double cream
2 eggs, beaten
2 (170g) tins of white crab meat in brine
2 red chillies, deseeded and very finely chopped
2cm (1 inch) fresh ginger, peeled and finely grated
8 spring onions, thinly sliced

TO SERVE

dressed green salad

Preheat the oven to 220°C/200°Cfan/gas 7 and put a large heavy baking sheet in the oven to get very hot.

First make the pastry, measure the flour, mustard and butter into a processor and whiz until it resembles breadcrumbs. Add the Parmesan and the egg, and whiz again until a dough forms.

Roll out and use the pastry to line two 4-hole Yorkshire pudding tin sheets.

Make the filling: measure the cream into a bowl and whisk with the eggs. Season with salt and pepper, then pour the mixture into the pastry cases.

Drain the crab meat and dry on kitchen paper. Tip into a bowl, mix with the rest of the filling ingredients and season with salt and pepper. Divide equally between the pastry cases.

Bake on the now very hot baking sheet for about 15–20 minutes until the pastry is golden brown and the filling is set.

● ***The tartlets can be made and baked a day ahead and reheated in a hot oven for about 8 minutes. They also freeze well once cooked.***

Serve warm with a dressed green salad.

AGA COOKING Slide on to the grid shelf on the floor of the roasting oven for about 15 minutes until the pastry is golden brown and the filling is set. Slide directly on the floor of the roasting oven for the last 5 of the 15 minutes to crisp up the underside of the pastry.

main *courses*

meat

This has become a regular favourite for our Sunday lunch. If you prefer the lamb really well done, lower the oven temperature at the end to 160°C/140°C fan/gas 3 and cook for a further hour.

PESTO-stuffed roast LEG of lamb

SERVES 6

1 boned leg of lamb, about 1.5kg (3lb), tied and ready to roast
2 tablespoons olive oil

FOR THE PESTO STUFFING

3 slices of white bread
grated zest and juice of 1 lemon
3 tablespoons green pesto
4 garlic cloves, peeled
1 tablespoon thyme leaves

FOR THE GRAVY

3–4 tablespoons flour
450ml (3/4 pint) good stock
300ml (1/2 pint) white wine
1–2 tablespoons redcurrant jelly
dash of gravy browning

First make the stuffing: break the bread into a food processor and whiz until it is fine breadcrumbs. Add the lemon zest, pesto, garlic and thyme leaves, and whiz again until combined and garlic is chopped. Season with salt and pepper. Expect the mixture to be very crumbly – it will hold together once pressed on to the lamb.

Using a very sharp knife, make deep cuts into the lamb, halfway through the lamb joint across the meatiest part of the leg, between the string that is tied around the lamb – about every 5cm (2 inches). Use the stuffing to fill the cuts (press down well with your hands) and season the leg with salt and pepper.

● ***The lamb can be prepared and stuffed up to 24 hours ahead, then kept covered in the fridge. It freezes well stuffed.***

Preheat the oven to 220°C/200°C fan/gas 7. Sit the lamb in a large roasting tin. Pour the lemon juice and oil over the lamb and rub them in a little. Roast in the preheated oven for about 20–30 minutes. Reduce the oven setting to 190°C/170C° fan/gas 5 and continue to roast for about 45 minutes. Remove from the oven, cover with foil and allow to rest for about 10–15 minutes while making the gravy.

Scrape up any juices from the roasting tin with a whisk; if necessary add a little more oil. Sprinkle in the flour and whisk together. Blend in the stock and wine, and bring to the boil over a high heat. Once it has thickened, whisk in the redcurrant jelly, season with salt and pepper and add a dash of gravy browning. Sieve into a warmed gravy jug.

Carve the lamb through each cut, removing the string as you go. Serve the lamb and stuffing with the hot gravy.

AGA COOKING To serve medium: slide on to the grid shelf on the floor of the roasting oven for about 45 minutes, cover loosely with foil if the top is getting too brown and transfer to the simmering oven for a further 45 minutes.
To serve well-done: cook as above in the roasting oven, but cook for 1 1/4–1 1/2 hours longer in the simmering oven.

If you prefer, this hearty warming casserole can be cooked slowly in the oven at 160°C/140°fan/gas 3 rather than cooking it on the hob.

BURFORD lamb SHANKS

SERVES 4

1 tablespoon oil
4 lamb shanks
40g (1 1/2 oz) butter
3 large onions, thinly sliced
40g (1 1/2 oz) flour
450ml (3/4 pint) beef stock
5 tablespoons red wine
2 tablespoons Worcestershire sauce
about 1 tablespoon redcurrant jelly

Heat the oil in a deep frying pan. Brown the lamb shanks in two batches until golden brown all over. Set aside.

Melt the butter in the pan, add the onions and cook over a low heat for about 5 minutes.

Add the flour to the onions, then blend in the stock, wine, Worcestershire sauce, redcurrant jelly and seasoning. Return the lamb shanks to the pan, cover, bring to the boil and then simmer for 2 1/2–3 hours, until the lamb is very tender and falling off the bone. (Halfway through cooking time, stir in 4–5 spoonfuls of water). Adjust the seasoning if necessary and add more redcurrant jelly if needed.

● ***This can be made completely the day before; reheat gently on the hob. It is not suitable for freezing.***

Serve with creamy mashed potatoes.

AGA COOKING Cook first on the boiling plate, cover and transfer to the simmering oven for about 2 1/2–3 hours, until the meat is falling off the bone.

This marinade can also be used for chicken or pork. You will need 8–10 kebab skewers. You can use metal or wooden ones – if using wooden ones, soak them in water beforehand as this prevents them from burning. These kebabs can also be cooked on the barbecue.

marinated LAMB kebabs

SERVES 4-6

800g ($1^3/_4$lb) boned leg lamb, trimmed of fat and diced into 2cm (1 inch) cubes
a little oil

FOR THE MARINADE

200g tub of full-fat Greek yoghurt
$1^1/_2$ tablespoons ground cumin
1 teaspoon ground turmeric
a few drops of Tabasco sauce
2 teaspoons soy sauce
2 tablespoons olive oil
2 tablespoons mango chutney

Mix all the marinade ingredients together in a bowl. Add the lamb and mix to coat the meat. Season with salt and pepper. Leave to marinate in the fridge for a few hours or overnight.

Thread about 5–6 of the lamb cubes on each skewer.

● ***The kebabs can be made completely and kept in the fridge until ready to cook. They are not suitable for freezing.***

Preheat the oven to 200°C/180°C fan/gas 6. Line a baking sheet with foil. Arrange the skewers on top and drizzle any remaining marinade and a little oil over the meat.

Bake in the oven for about 15 minutes, until golden brown and cooked through.

Serve hot with a Vegetable Kebab (page 115) or dressed salad.

AGA COOKING Slide the baking sheet on the top set of runners in the roasting oven for about 15 minutes until golden brown and cooked through.

This is the simplest small roast – the prime cut of lamb, loin is expensive but guaranteed to be tender as long as it is not overcooked. Being very lean, there is no waste and it is easy to carve.

St GEORGE's minted lamb

SERVES 4–6

2 small lamb loin fillets, each about 350g (12oz)
olive oil
2 teaspoons redcurrant jelly
2 teaspoons mint sauce

FOR THE MINT GRAVY

good knob of butter
1 level tablespoon flour
200ml (7fl oz) stock
100ml (3fl oz) red wine
1 teaspoon redcurrant jelly
1 tablespoon chopped fresh mint

Heat a non-stick frying pan over a high heat.

Roll each lamb loin in a little oil and season with salt and pepper. Brown each side of each fillet in the hot frying pan for about 30 seconds until golden brown.

Mix together the redcurrant jelly and mint sauce, and spread over the top of the fillet.

● ***The fillets can be prepared up to this stage 12 hours ahead, as can the sauce. They are not suitable for freezing.***

Preheat the oven to 200°C/180°C fan/gas 6 and roast the fillets for about 10 minutes, until still pink in the middle.

Make the mint gravy in the unwashed frying pan (if not making ahead): melt the butter and whisk in the flour to make a thin roux. Blend in the stock and wine, whisk and bring to the boil. Whisk in the redcurrant jelly, season with salt and pepper, and add fresh mint.

Carve the lamb fillets into thick slices and serve with the mint gravy.

AGA COOKING Fry the fillets in a non-stick frying pan on the boiling plate. Roast on the top set of runners in the roasting oven for about 8 minutes.

The honey and mustard not only add flavour to the chops but give it a golden-brown finish. The sauce is optional – my family love sauce!

honey and mustard glazed PORK chops

SERVES 4

4 pork chops

FOR THE MARINADE

3 tablespoons grainy mustard
1 tablespoon runny honey
2 tablespoons sunflower oil
juice of 1/2 lemon
about 12 fresh sage leaves, chopped, or 1 teaspoon dried sage

FOR THE SAUCE

1/2 onion, finely chopped
5 tablespoons apple juice
150ml (1/4 pint) double cream
2 tablespoons chopped parsley

Trim any surplus fat from the chops. Snip the fat edge with scissors at 1cm (1/2 inch) intervals. Season with salt and pepper.

Measure the marinade ingredients into a large shallow dish (big enough for the chops to lay flat), mix together and season with salt and pepper. Toss the chops in the marinade and leave for 30 minutes-2 hours.

● ***The chops can be marinated up to 2 hours ahead. They are not suitable for freezing.***

When ready to serve, preheat the grill to high. Line the grill pan with foil and replace the rack. Lift the chops out of the marinade and reserve the liquid. Grill the chops for about 15 minutes, until cooked through, turning halfway. Keep the cooked chops warm and reserve the juices for the sauce.

To make the sauce, pour the reserved juices and marinade into a small pan, add the onion and apple juice, and boil rapidly until reduced by half. Add the cream, season and bring to boil. Add the parsley and adjust the seasoning if necessary. Serve with the chops and some mashed potato.

AGA COOKING Cook the chops on a preheated griddle pan or frying pan on the boiling plate.

This casserole is great for a party as it can be scaled up readily and, being hot and spicy, is especially popular with the younger generation.

pepperpot PORK

SERVES 6

225g (8oz) chorizo sausage, skin removed and sliced into rounds
750g (1 1/2 lb) pork leg, cut into 2cm (1 inch) cubes
2 large onions, thinly sliced
3 garlic cloves, crushed
1 tablespoon paprika
150ml (1/4 pint) dry sherry
two 400g cans of chopped tomatoes
1 teaspoon sugar
75g (3oz) small black olives, pitted

Preheat the oven to 160°C/140°C fan/gas 3.

Heat a large ovenproof casserole dish. Add the chorizo and fry over a high heat until lightly browned and the oil has started to come out of the sausage. Remove the sausage with a slotted spoon and put on a plate. Brown the pork in the chorizo oil; you will need to do this in two batches. Transfer to the chorizo plate.

Add the onions and garlic to the pan and stir until the onions are beginning to soften, add the paprika, then blend in the sherry and tomatoes. Season with salt and pepper, and add the sugar. Bring to the boil and return the pork and sausage to the pan, then cover and transfer to the preheated oven for about 2 hours until tender.

● ***This can be made up to 2 days ahead and reheated gently. It may also be frozen for up to 2 months – any longer and the spicy sausage will overpower the flavour of the sauce.***

Stir in the olives and serve with boiled rice.

AGA COOKING Make on the boiling plate, bring to the boil, cover and transfer to the simmering oven for about 2–3 hours until tender.

This is a very fashionable recipe at the moment – all the restaurants are serving it! For a modern variation, rub some Chinese five-spice powder into the skin before crisping it up at the end.

slow-roast belly of PORK *with onion gravy*

SERVES 6

1 large onion, chopped
1 tablespoon oil
1.2kg (2½ lb) boned belly of pork, skin scored by the butcher
sea salt
2–3 tablespoons flour
600ml (1 pint) stock
1 tablespoon apple jelly or redcurrant jelly
dash of gravy browning

Put the onion and oil in the base of a small roasting tin. Put a small grill rack on top and place the belly, skin side up, on the rack. Rub the sea salt into the scored skin.

● ***The pork belly can be prepared to this point and kept in the refrigerator for up to 8 hours. It cannot be frozen.***

Slow-roast the pork in an oven preheated to 160°C/140°C fan/gas 3 for about 2–2½ hours. Turn up the heat to 220°C/200°C fan/gas 7 and roast for about 30–40 minutes more, or until the skin has become crisp and the onions have turned golden brown. (Keep an eye on the onion – if it starts to catch and burn at any point, then tuck it under the pork.) Transfer the belly to a plate to rest while you make the gravy.

Add the flour to the onion and fat in the bottom of the tin and mix together with a wooden spoon. Put the tin on the hob and blend in the stock and jelly over a medium heat. Bring up to the boil and simmer for a few minutes. Season with a little salt and pepper, and add a dash of gravy browning if you like a darker gravy.

Remove the crackling from the top of the roast and slice the pork. Snip the crackling into pieces and arrange pork and crackling on a plate. Serve with the gravy and some mashed sweet potatoes.

AGA COOKING Slow-roast the belly in the simmering oven for about 4 hours. Transfer to the top of the roasting oven for a further 30 minutes, until the skin is crisp and crackling.

This pork loin has a superb green stuffing without needing to be tied up with string that must be removed at the end, as the loin is hollowed out to take the stuffing. If the crackling is not really crisp when the pork is done, lift the pork on to a plate to rest, then slice off the crackling with a sharp knife and return it to a very hot oven on a rack in the roasting tin for a further 10 minutes to crisp up.

LOIN of pork with leek stuffing

and rich apple gravy

SERVES 6

1.7kg ($3^{1}/_{2}$lb) boned loin of pork, skin scored
a little oil

FOR THE LEEK STUFFING

a little oil or butter
1 medium leek, thinly sliced
2 fat pork sausages
3 heaped tablespoons chopped parsley

FOR THE RICH APPLE GRAVY

1 level tablespoon flour
300ml ($^{1}/_{2}$ pint) chicken or game stock
3 tablespoons medium sherry
a little redcurrant jelly
$^{1}/_{2}$ cooking apple, peeled, cored and grated

First make the stuffing. Melt a little oil or butter in a large pan, add the leek and fry it gently until softened. Season with salt and pepper and set aside until cold.

When the leeks are cold, skin the sausages, then mix the sausage meat and parsley into the leeks (it is easiest to do this with your hands).

Make a deep incision through the eye of the pork loin with a sharp knife, turning it to make a tunnel. Stuff the tunnel with the leek mixture, packing it in with your fingers.

● ***The loin the can now be kept in the fridge for up to 24 hours before roasting. It is not suitable for freezing.***

When ready to serve, preheat the oven to 200°C/180°C fan/gas 6. Put the joint in a roasting tin, rub the skin with a little oil and season with lots of sea salt. Roast in the preheated oven for about $1^{1}/_{2}$ hours, until the juices run clear.

Transfer the pork to a serving plate, cover with foil and allow to rest. Carefully spoon off a tablespoon of the fat from the roasting tin and discard. Add the flour to the tin, heat over a low heat and whisk until smooth. Add the stock, sherry, redcurrant jelly and apple, as well as any juices from rested pork, then whisk again while bringing to the boil. Season to taste.

Carve the pork and serve with the crackling and gravy.

AGA COOKING Roast on the second set of runners in the roasting oven for about $1^{1}/_{4}$-$1^{1}/_{2}$ hours until crisp.

This stew freezes very well and, like most stews, it improves in flavour if made in advance. The chocolate enriches the casserole. If you can't get frozen chestnuts, use 100g (4oz) dried chestnuts and soak them overnight before frying. If you have a problem finding pancetta lardons, use smoked bacon lardons instead.

BURLINGTON beef

SERVES 6

2 tablespoons sunflower oil, plus a little more for the chestnuts
900g (2 lb) stewing beef, cut into 2 cm (1 inch) cubes
75g (3 oz) raw pancetta lardons
2 large onions, coarsely chopped
2 fat garlic cloves, crushed
2 level tablespoons plain flour
300 ml (1/2 pint) chicken stock
300 ml (1/2 pint) red wine
1 small celeriac, peeled and cut 2 cm (1 inch) cubes
2 sprigs of thyme
200g (7 oz) frozen chestnuts, defrosted and cut in half
8 squares of dark chocolate
2 tablespoons chopped parsley

Preheat the oven to 160°C/140°C fan/gas 3.

Heat the oil in a pan which has a lid or in a casserole and brown the beef in batches over a high heat. Transfer to a plate. Add the pancetta lardons to the pan and fry until golden brown, then put them on the plate with the browned beef.

Add the onions and garlic to the pan and fry in the fat in the pan that has been left from the pancetta for about 3–4 minutes. Blend in the flour and stir in the stock and red wine.

Return the beef and pancetta lardons to the pan with any juices, then add the celeriac. Season to taste and add the thyme sprigs. Bring to the boil, cover with the lid and transfer to the oven for about 2–2 1/2 hours until the beef is tender.

About 30 minutes before the end of the cooking time, fry the chestnuts in a little oil until golden brown and add to the casserole. Remove the sprigs of thyme.

● ***This can be made up to this stage up to 2 days ahead and reheated. It also freezes well.***

When the stew is ready, stir in the chocolate until melted, sprinkle with parsley and serve with creamy mashed potatoes or rice.

AGA COOKING Bring to the boil on the boiling plate, cover and transfer to the simmering oven for about 3–3 1/2 hours, until the beef is tender.

This dish is so quick to make and quite delicious. It's on the chilli-hot side, so go steady with the Thai paste. It is very trendy to serve each person with a bowl of stir-fry alongside a bowl of rice.

quick THAI COCONUT beef stir-fry

SERVES 6

- 350g (12oz) rump beef steak
- 2 tablespoons oil
- 1 bunch of spring onions, thinly sliced (keep the white parts and the green ends separate)
- 1 red pepper, deseeded and thinly sliced
- 1 tablespoon green Thai paste
- 150g (5oz) shiitake mushrooms, halved
- 225g can of bamboo shoots, drained
- 400ml can of coconut milk
- 1 tablespoon brown sugar
- grated zest and juice of 1 lime
- 150g (5oz) mangetout, thinly sliced

● ***All the ingredients can be prepared up to a day ahead and kept in the fridge. They are not suitable for freezing.***

Trim any surplus fat from the steak and beat it out between two pieces of cling film, using a wooden rolling pin, until 1cm (1/2 inch) thick. Slice into thin strips.

Heat 1 tablespoon of oil in a frying pan. Brown the beef very quickly in two batches. Set aside. Add the remaining oil and the white parts from the spring onions, the red pepper and the Thai paste to the pan, and stir-fry for a few seconds.

Add the mushrooms, bamboo shoots, coconut milk, sugar and lime zest and juice. Bring to the boil and simmer for about 5 minutes.

Add the mangetout and return the beef to the pan, and then simmer for another 3 minutes. Check the seasoning and adjust if necessary. Sprinkle the green parts from the spring onions over the top.

Turn into warmed bowls and serve with boiled rice.

AGA COOKING Stir-fry on the boiling plate.

Memories of the 1960s, when this dish was all the rage – cooked on a spirit stove in front of you in the most posh restaurants. I do it for a special treat on a Saturday night. You'll find 4–6 steaks fit nicely into a large frying pan. I don't beat the steaks out like escalopes – I prefer just to flatten them with my hand to about 1cm (1/2 inch) thick – it is then easier to get them brown on the outside but stay pink in the middle.

fillet STEAK with DIANE sauce

SERVES 4–6

4–6 centre-cut fillet steaks each about 150g (5oz)
40g (1 1/2 oz) butter

FOR THE DIANE SAUCE

1 large onion, very finely chopped
2 tablespoons brandy
1 tablespoon Dijon mustard
1 tablespoon Worcestershire sauce
150ml (1/4 pint) double cream
a little water or stock
2 tablespoons chopped fresh parsley

Flatten each steak with the palm of the hand to a thickness of 1cm (1/2 inch). Spread one side of each steak with a little of the butter and season with salt and pepper.

Heat a large non stick frying pan until piping-hot. Drop the steaks into the pan and cook over a high heat for 1 minute on each side – you may need to add a little more of the butter when cooking the second sides. Lift out and keep warm or allow to rest if serving immediately.

Next make the sauce: add the remaining butter to the pan, add the onion and cook gently until softened and tender. Add the brandy, mustard, Worcestershire sauce and cream, bring to the boil and season with salt and pepper. You may need to add a little water or stock so that the sauce is the thickness of pouring cream. Stir in half the parsley.

● ***To prepare ahead, lift the steaks out on to a metal baking tray lined with foil, allow to cool, cover and refrigerate together with the made sauce (without the parsley) for up to 12 hours ahead. Reheat the steaks uncovered in a very hot oven (220°C/200°C fan/gas 6) for 8 minutes. Add any cooking juices to the sauce and serve.***

Serve the steaks with the sauce and sprinkled with remaining parsley, accompanied by rösti potatoes (page 123).

AGA COOKING Fry the steaks on the boiling plate, reheat on the second set of runners in the roasting oven for 8 minutes and reheat the sauce on the boiling plate.

The great plus point of this recipe is that you don't have to brown the meatballs, which you often have to do in many recipes, and they are also really tasty. Take care not to stir the meatballs when cooking, as they could fall apart. Known as polpette in Italy, they are popular family fare there, and a common way of using up leftovers. We often serve them with cooked pasta ribbons, as here.

ITALIAN meatballs *with Parmesan and lemon*

SERVES 4–6

FOR THE MEATBALLS

450g (1 lb) raw lean minced beef
25g (1oz) fresh breadcrumbs
2 garlic cloves, crushed
50g (2 oz) Parmesan cheese, grated
1 egg yolk
3 tablespoons green pesto
grated zest and juice of 1 lemon

FOR THE TOMATO SAUCE

1 tablespoon oil
1 onion, roughly chopped
2 celery stalks, thinly sliced
1 garlic clove, crushed
1 teaspoon sugar
1 (500ml) carton of passata

TO SERVE

2 tablespoons chopped fresh parsley
shavings of Parmesan to serve (optional)

To make the meatballs, measure all the ingredients into a bowl with salt and pepper to taste, and mix together gently with your hands – do not overwork or your meatballs will be heavy. Shape into 24 round balls, put on a plate and leave in the fridge.

To make the sauce, heat the oil in a shallow wide-based pan, add the onion and celery, and fry for few minutes over a high heat. Cover and simmer over a low heat for about 15 minutes until soft. Return the pan to the heat, and add the garlic, sugar and passata. Bring to the boil and season to taste.

● ***Shape the meatballs up to 24 hours ahead. They freeze well raw. The sauce can be made up to 3 days ahead.***

Preheat the oven to 180°C/160°C fan/gas 4. Drop the meatballs into the hot sauce and coat well. Cover with a lid and slide into the preheated oven for about 25 minutes.

Sprinkle with parsley and Parmesan shavings to serve.

AGA COOKING Add onion and celery for sauce to the oil, fry briefly on boiling plate, cover and transfer to simmering oven for about 15 minutes, until soft. Add meatballs, bring to boil, cover and return to simmering oven for about an hour.

Here boned chicken thighs are coated with a crisp spicy pecan crust. Some of the nuts may fall off – don't worry, just sprinkle them back over the chicken when serving them warm, with potato wedges and a dressed salad.

baked pecan CHICKEN

SERVES 4

6–8 chicken thighs, boned and skin removed

FOR THE PECAN CRUST

2 tablespoons orange juice from a carton
2 tablespoons Dijon mustard
2 tablespoons oil
1/2 teaspoon curry powder
2 tablespoons smooth mango chutney
100g (4oz) pecan nuts, finely chopped
paprika

Make the pecan crust by mixing all the ingredients except the paprika in a bowl until well combined.

Line a roasting tin with parchment paper and spread the mixture over the top.

Season the chicken with salt and pepper and press the thighs into the crust mixture on both sides, so each thigh is coated with a thin layer.

Arrange in a single layer in the roasting tin and sprinkle with a little paprika.

● ***The chicken can be rolled in the crumb mixture up to 24 hours ahead and kept covered in the fridge. It is not suitable for freezing.***

Bake in an oven preheated to 200°C/180°C fan/gas 6 for about 30 minutes, until golden brown and crispy.

AGA COOKING Slide on to the second set of runners in the roasting oven for about 25–30 minutes.

poultry and game

I first had this combination in South Africa and it has since become a firm favourite. It is worth using fresh pears. I find the cloudy apple juice not too dry and the best for this. It is so simple to make – as there is no pre-frying of the chicken breasts. I cooked it for my mother on her 100th birthday – she loves fruit with chicken, and it has a hint of spice too.

chicken with CALVADOS *and poached pears*

SERVES 6

- 6 small boneless, skinless chicken breasts
- 3 tablespoons Calvados or brandy
- generous 25g (1oz) butter
- 25g (1oz) flour
- 1 teaspoon medium curry powder
- 450ml (3/4 pint) apple juice
- 3 just-ripe pears, peeled, cored and sliced in half lengthways
- 3 tablespoons double cream
- juice of 1/2 lemon
- 2 tablespoons chopped fresh parsley

Marinate the chicken breasts in the Calvados or brandy for at least 1 hour, preferably overnight.

Melt the butter in a large shallow saucepan. Add the flour and curry powder, and stir over a medium heat for a few seconds. Blend in the apple juice and bring to the boil until the sauce has thickened.

Add the chicken breasts, Calvados and pears, season with salt and pepper, cover with a lid and simmer over a low heat for about 15 minutes, until the chicken breasts are cooked through, turning the chicken and pears over halfway through.

● ***This can be made to this point up to 24 hours ahead, then kept covered in the fridge. Gently reheat and continue as below. This is not suitable for freezing.***

Stir in the double cream and lemon juice, and heat through gently until the chicken is piping hot.

Carve each chicken breast into 4 slices and slice the pears thickly widthways. Arrange on plates and pour over the hot sauce (expect plenty of sauce), then sprinkle with parsley and serve with mashed potatoes or rice.

AGA COOKING Bring to the boil on the boiling plate, cover and transfer to the simmering oven for about 25 minutes, until the chicken is cooked through.

I have long praised chicken thighs as being the best cut of the chicken. If you slightly overcook them, all the better. Peppadew peppers are small sweet bell peppers sold in jars.

CHICKEN with lemon grass and ginger

SERVES 4–6

1 tablespoon oil
2 large onions, thinly sliced
2 garlic cloves, crushed
6cm (3 inches) fresh ginger, peeled and roughly chopped
8 Peppadew peppers (see above)
grated zest and juice of 1/2 lemon
2 teaspoons ground coriander seeds
1 rounded tablespoon cornflour
300ml (1/2 pint) chicken stock
8 chicken thighs, skinned and boned
1 piece of lemon grass, bashed
5 tablespoons double cream

Heat the oil in a large non stick-frying pan. Add the onions, fry for 2–3 minutes, cover with a lid and simmer over a low heat until they are soft and tender.

Put the garlic, ginger, peppers, lemon zest and juice, coriander and cornflour in a food processor and whiz to a smooth paste (or crush using a pestle and mortar).

Add the paste to the onions and stir over the heat, then blend in the stock. Add the chicken thighs and lemon grass, and season with salt and pepper. Cover and simmer for about 45 minutes over a low heat or in an oven preheated to 160°C/140°C fan/gas 3.

When the chicken is tender, lift out the lemon grass and discard.

● ***This can be made up to this stage up to 48 hours ahead, kept covered in the fridge. It also freezes well.***

Just before serving, add the cream. Check the seasoning and adjust if necessary. Bring to the boil and serve with rice or mashed potatoes.

AGA COOKING Make in an ovenproof pan on the boiling plate, cover and transfer to the simmering oven for about 45 minutes, until the chicken is cooked through.

This treatment is also excellent with pheasant breasts, but the cooking time may be slightly less as they're smaller. If your chicken breasts are large, you can carve enough slices at an angle from 2 breasts to serve 3 people. For a large party, pre-brown the chilled wrapped breasts in a very hot pan well ahead and then finish in the oven later.

PORCINI-stuffed chicken

SERVES 6

25 g (1 oz) dried porcini mushrooms
300 ml (1/2 pint) boiling water
75 g (3 oz) butter, softened
2 large garlic cloves, crushed, plus more for the roasting tin
small bunch of basil, chopped
6 small boneless, skinless chicken breasts
12 thin rashers of streaky bacon, stretched if necessary
2 tablespoons chopped parsley

FOR THE PORT AND PARSLEY SAUCE

1–2 tablespoons Worcestershire sauce
3 tablespoons port
1 heaped teaspoon cornflour
200 ml tub of full-fat crème fraîche

Measure the dried mushrooms into a bowl and pour over the 300ml boiling water. Leave for about 20 minutes.

In a bowl, mix together the butter, garlic and 3 tablespoons of the basil. Season with salt and pepper. Strain the mushrooms, reserving the liquid, and chop the mushrooms fairly finely. Mix with the butter mixture.

Using a sharp knife, cut a pocket horizontally through the thick part of each chicken breast, almost through to the other side.

Divide the mushroom stuffing into six and stuff some into each pocket. Season the chicken breasts and wrap 2 slices of bacon around each one.

● ***The chicken can be stuffed and rolled up to 24 hours ahead, and kept in the fridge. The sauce can be prepared ahead and kept in the same way, then finished in the roasting pan. You can freeze the raw chicken for up to one month; thaw carefully before cooking.***

Sit the pieces in a buttered roasting tin and roast for about 15–20 minutes in an oven preheated to 220°C/200°C fan/gas 7 until cooked through and crisp. Allow to rest while making the sauce.

Skim any fat from the roasting tin, then make the sauce. Pour the reserved mushroom liquid into the roasting tin and mix with the cooking juices. Add the Worcestershire sauce and port, and reduce by half on the hob. Mix the cornflour with about 3 tablespoons of the crème fraîche and blend till smooth. Add to the rest of the crème fraîche, then quickly stir into the mushroom liquid in the pan, check and adjust seasoning, if necessary, and bring to the boil.

Carve each breast carefully at an angle into 3–5 slices, arrange on a plate and serve with a little sauce. Sprinkle with parsley and serve any remaining sauce separately. If in a hurry, leave the breasts whole. Serve with spinach.

AGA COOKING Slide the tray on to the top set of runners in the roasting oven for about 15 minutes, until the chicken is cooked through and the bacon is crisp.

Served with rice, this is a perfect light and fresh supper dish for family or friends. If you prefer, use skinless, boneless chicken thighs, but they may need longer cooking.

pan-fried chicken *with spiced mango sauce*

SERVES 6

4 small skinless, boneless chicken breasts
about 1 tablespoon sunflower oil
1 tablespoon runny honey
2 tablespoons chopped parsley

FOR THE SPICED MANGO SAUCE

1 large mango
6 mild Peppadew peppers from a jar (see page 71)
3 tablespoons mango chutney
150 g (5 oz) Greek yoghurt
2 teaspoons Chinese five-spice powder
2 teaspoons flour
juice of 1/2 lemon

First, make the sauce: cut the mango in half lengthways, either side of the stone. Peel the fruit and cut the flesh into manageable-sized pieces. Measure half the mango into a processor, choosing the less even pieces. Add the peppers, chutney, yoghurt, five-spice powder, flour and lemon juice, and whiz until fairly smooth. Season.

● ***The sauce can be made up to 48 hours ahead and kept in the fridge. This dish is not suitable for freezing.***

Cut the chicken breasts into pencil-thin strips and season with salt and pepper. Heat a large non-stick frying pan over a high heat. Add the oil and chicken strips, spread evenly around the pan and pour over the honey. Fry briskly over a high heat for 2–3 minutes, until the chicken is browned and just cooked (if you have only a small frying pan, you will need to do this in 2 batches).

Pour the sauce over the chicken in the pan and stir until it has thickened and is bubbling. Stir in the reserved mango and adjust the seasoning if necessary. Turn out into a warmed serving dish and sprinkle with the parsley.

AGA COOKING Heat a large non-stick frying pan on the boiling plate until piping hot and continue with the recipe.

This is a very smart way of cooking chicken breasts. You can now buy smooth mango chutney (with no bits). If you only have the traditional mango chutney for the glaze, that's fine, just avoid the bits.

roasted chicken breasts *with mango glaze*

SERVES 6

butter, for the roasting tin
2 tablespoons olive oil
1 very large onion, finely chopped
100 g (4 oz) bacon lardons or chopped streaky bacon
100 g (4 oz) spinach, chopped
leaves from a large sprig of thyme
6 small boneless chicken breasts, with skin on
about 2 tablespoons smooth mango chutney
a little paprika
chopped parsley to serve (optional)

FOR THE SAUCE

25 g (1 oz) butter
1 heaped teaspoon flour
100 ml (3 fl oz) Madeira or port
300 ml (1/2 pint) cranberry juice
2 tablespoons smooth mango chutney

Butter and season a roasting tin large enough that the chicken breasts will have plenty of room around them.

Heat the oil in a large non-stick frying pan and add the onion. Fry for a few minutes, stir in the bacon, then continue to fry over a low heat for about 10 minutes until tender. Add the spinach, stirring continually, until it is just wilted and any liquid is driven off. Season and stir in thyme leaves.

Cut each chicken breast in half horizontally (keeping them in pairs). Place the bottom halves in the roasting tin and season. Divide the spinach mixture between each and top with the other piece of chicken, skin side uppermost. Spread mango chutney over the skin of each breast and sprinkle with a little paprika.

● ***The chicken can be totally prepared ahead and left in the fridge covered with cling film up to 24 hours ahead. The sauce can also be made ahead in a pan rather than the roasting tin – it will be pale in colour but once reheated and the juices from the roasting tin are added it will be a good colour.***

Cook in an oven preheated to 220°C/200°C fan/gas 7 for about 20 minutes, until the chicken is cooked through. Remove from the tin and keep warm.

To make the sauce: add the butter to the tin with all the chicken juices and melt it over a low heat. Whisk in the flour, add the Madeira and cranberry juice, slowly whisking, and bring to the boil. Add the mango chutney and reduce a little over a high heat. Check and adjust the seasoning, if necessary.

As you serve the chicken, slide the top slice slightly to the side to reveal the lovely green filling. Pour the sauce around the chicken and sprinkle with parsley, if you like.

AGA COOKING Soften the bacon and onion in the simmering oven for about 15 minutes until tender. Drive off any liquid on the boiling plate and continue as above. Roast the chicken at the top of the roasting oven for about 15–20 minutes until just done; keep warm in the simmering oven while making the sauce.

This duck recipe is remarkably simple, as it is slow-roasted for most of the time – which also makes it very tender. Use orange juice from a carton.

orange-glazed crispy DUCK

pictured on page 76-7

SERVES 4

2.5kg (5lb) oven-ready duck
3 tablespoons thick-cut orange marmalade

FOR THE SAUCE

1 tablespoon cornflour
150ml (1/4 pint) red wine
300ml (1/2 pint) orange juice
3 tablespoons soy sauce

Preheat the oven to 220°C/200C°fan/gas 7.

Put the duck upside down on a large rack in a roasting tin. Roast in the oven for 30 minutes, then carefully turn the duck the right way up and roast for another 30 minutes. Turn the oven setting down to 160°C/140C°fan/gas 3 and cook for a further 1–1 1/2 hours until the duck is just cooked through.

Increase the oven setting again to 220°C/200°C fan/gas 6. Spread the marmalade over the top of the duck and pop the bird back in the oven for about 5–10 minutes to crisp up the skin. Watch very carefully to ensure that the duck does not become too brown.

Make the sauce: mix the cornflour in a little bowl with 2 tablespoons of water. Measure the red wine, orange juice and soy sauce into a saucepan. Bring to the boil, then simmer and add the slaked cornflour, stirring until it has thickened. Check and adjust the seasoning, if necessary.

● ***Serve the duck immediately. The sauce can be made up to a day ahead and whisked into the skimmed juices from the tin.***

Skim off as much fat from the pan juices as you can and then stir the sauce into the skimmed juices in the roasting tin.

Joint the duck into 4 and serve with the sauce and some stir-fried greens.

AGA COOKING Cook the duck in the roasting oven for about 50 minutes until brown all over, then transfer to the simmering oven for about 1 1/2 hours until just cooked through.

It amazes me why more people don't serve quail more often. It can be bought boned from good butchers or supermarkets, prepared ahead and involves no last-minute carving. This makes a wonderful dinner party dish and is not nearly as expensive as those using many other quality meats.

roast stuffed QUAIL
with tomato and thyme sauce

SERVES 4–6

8 boned quails
8 slices of Italian cured ham
a little runny honey to glaze

FOR THE MUSHROOM STUFFING

50g (2oz) butter
2 shallots, finely chopped
100g (4oz) button mushrooms, finely chopped
4 good tablespoons thyme leaves
25g (1oz) fresh white breadcrumbs
1 egg yolk

FOR THE SUN-DRIED TOMATO AND THYME SAUCE

300ml (1/2 pint) double cream
2 tablespoons sun-dried tomato paste
2 good tablespoons thyme leaves

For the mushroom stuffing, melt the butter in a pan, add the shallots and mushrooms, and fry for a few minutes over a high heat. Tip into a bowl, add the thyme leaves, breadcrumbs, egg yolk and season with salt and pepper. Stir well.

To stuff the quail, lay the birds breast side down on the chopping board, season with salt and pepper, and fill the cavity of each bird with the stuffing. Put the birds together to reshape. Turn them the right way up and arrange in a roasting tin. Lay a piece of cured ham on the breast of each bird and brush with a little honey.

● ***The birds can be stuffed and ready for the oven up to 48 hours ahead. They also freeze well.***

Roast in an oven preheated to 200°C/180°C fan/gas 6 for about 15–20 minutes, until crisp, golden brown and cooked right through. Set aside to rest while making the sauce.

To make the sauce, pour the cream into the roasting tin and whisk with the quail cooking juices. Boil for a few minutes over a high heat and stir in the tomato paste and thyme leaves. Season with salt and pepper.

Serve one or two quail per person, with a little of the sauce.

AGA COOKING Cook the quails on the top of the roasting oven for about 15 minutes, until crisp, golden brown and cooked right through.

So often recipes for pheasant are in a brown gravy or creamy sauce. This makes a pleasant change to have a mix of peppers, tomatoes, onion and garlic. If you are an olive lover, a few black olives can also be added. Take care not to overcook the pheasant breasts; they really will only take 15–20 minutes.

caledonian PHEASANT

with cauliflower and onion purée

SERVES 6

3 red peppers
100g (4oz) pancetta lardons
1 tablespoon oil
1 large onion, roughly chopped
1–2 garlic cloves, crushed
1/2–1 tablespoon paprika
400g (14oz) tin of chopped tomatoes
6 pheasant breasts, skinned
1–2 tablespoons chopped parsley

FOR THE CAULIFLOWER AND ONION PUREE

1 medium cauliflower
1/2 large onion, finely chopped
4–6 level tablespoons full-fat crème fraîche

Preheat a hot grill. Cut the peppers in half, remove the seeds and place the halves, cut side down, on a baking sheet. Grill until the skins are black. Transfer the charred peppers to a polythene bag and leave until cold enough to handle, then peel off their skins and slice the flesh into thick strips.

While the peppers are cooling, start making the cauliflower and onion purée: remove the outside leaves from the cauliflower and separate the florets. Put in a pan with the onion and cover with salted water. Boil until just tender, drain thoroughly and return to the pan to dry off as much as possible.

Meanwhile, fry the lardons in a dry hot non-stick frying pan until crisp, then transfer to a plate. Add the oil to the pan if necessary and cook the onion until soft. Add the garlic and paprika, and cook for 2 minutes.

Add the tomatoes, pancetta, peppers and pheasant breasts, cover and bring to the boil. Simmer gently for 15–20 minutes, until the breasts are cooked through and tender. Add a little stock or water if the sauce gets too thick.

While the pheasant is cooking, finish the purée: transfer the cauliflower to a food processor and purée until very smooth. You will have to stop the machine a couple of times to scrape it down the sides. When velvety smooth, add the crème fraîche and season. Reheat gently if necessary.

● ***The pheasant can be cooked up to 2 days ahead and reheated to serve. It also freezes well. The purée can be made up to 8 hours ahead and reheated in a pan, or simply kept warm for half an hour or so.***

Sprinkle with parsley before serving hot with mashed potato.

AGA COOKING Char the peppers on the top set of runners in the roasting oven for about 15 minutes. Continue as above, bring to the boil, cover and transfer to the simmering oven for about 15–20 minutes until tender.

This pie goes well with a celeriac purée and red cabbage. You can simplify things by just serving the hot pie filling as a game casserole. If you do, sprinkle it with some chopped parsley and, if you like, thinly slice another small orange and garnish the plates with them. The casserole suits the same accompaniments as the pie.

GAME PIE with leeks and orange

SERVES 4–6

750g (1½lb) boneless mixed game
50g (2oz) butter
200g (7oz) smoked bacon lardons
25g (1oz) flour
150ml (¼ pint) red wine
300ml (½ pint) chicken stock
2 tablespoons redcurrant jelly, plus more to serve
1 very small orange
1 large leek, quartered lengthways then cut across into 1cm (½ inch pieces)
450g (1lb) puff pastry (look out for butter puff pastry, which has much better flavour)
a little beaten egg and milk to glaze

Preheat the oven to 160°C/140°C fan/gas 3. Cut the game into manageable pieces, removing any fat, skin or sinew. Melt half the butter in a large non-stick frying pan and brown the game and bacon over a high heat until sealed all over (you may need to do this in two batches). Remove with a slotted spoon and set aside.

Add the remaining butter to the frying pan, allow it to melt, then sprinkle in the flour and cook for a few moments. Gradually blend in the wine, allow to thicken, then add the stock and redcurrant jelly. Bring to the boil, stirring, season and add one whole orange. Return the game and bacon to the pan.

Turn into an ovenproof casserole, cover and cook in the oven for about 2 hours. About 15 minutes before the end of cooking, add the leek.

After the 2 hours, lift the softened orange into a sieve, cut it in half, stand it over a bowl and push through the sieve, collecting the juices. Gradually stir into the stew until the taste is perfect and adjust the seasoning. If the liquid is still a little thick, add a little stock or water. Set aside to cool.

Preheat the oven to 200°C/180°C fan/gas 6. Roll out the pastry to a suitable shape to cover a 1.5 litre (2½ pint) pie dish and cut a strip of pastry from the trimmings to go all the way round the rim of the dish. Put the cooled filling in the dish, moisten the rim with water and press the pastry strip in place all round. Sit the pastry cover in place and press it down on the pastry strip. Decorate with leaves cut from the trimmings if you like. Glaze the pastry with the egg and milk mixture and cook in the oven for 20–30 minutes until the pastry is well risen and coloured and the filling is bubbling.

● ***The pie can be made up to 2 days ahead and left unbaked in the fridge or frozen. Thaw if necessary and cook as above.***

Serve with more redcurrant jelly, celeriac purée and red cabbage.

AGA COOKING Make filling on boiling plate, bring to the boil, cover and transfer to simmering oven for about 2 hours, until the game is tender. Make the pie as above. Bake on second set of runners in the roasting oven for about 25 minutes.

Venison has a wonderful flavour and is virtually fat-free, but you need to be careful not to overcook it. It is always useful to have a can of condensed consommé in the larder, as it makes an excellent stock. When buying a boned loin of venison, ask the butcher for the middle cut and don't worry if it seems thin, as it actually bulks up on cooking.

peppered VENISON

SERVES 6

450g (1 lb) boned loin of venison
3 tablespoons olive oil
1 teaspoon chopped fresh thyme leaves
1 tablespoon cracked black pepper

FOR THE SAUCE

1 tablespoon olive oil
1 shallot, finely chopped
½ teaspoon grated fresh ginger
1 (295 ml) can of condensed beef consommé
1 level tablespoon cornflour
1 good tablespoon redcurrant jelly, plus more to serve
1 teaspoon balsamic vinegar

Trim any membrane from the loin. Rub the oil, thyme and a little pepper well into the meat and leave (overnight if time allows) to marinate.

Heat a dry frying pan until hot. Lightly roll the loin in the cracked pepper and brown very quickly in the hot pan, then transfer to a small roasting tin until ready to serve.

To make the sauce, add the oil, shallot and ginger to the unwashed frying pan and sauté the shallots until soft. Pour in the consommé and bring to the boil. Mix the cornflour with a few tablespoons of water and pour into the pan, then stir while the sauce thickens. Add the redcurrant jelly and balsamic vinegar. Check and adjust the seasoning if necessary.

● ***The venison can be browned up to 12 hours ahead. The sauce can be made up to 24 hours ahead. Neither is suitable for freezing.***

Roast the venison for about 12 minutes in an oven preheated to 220°C/200°C fan/gas 7 (a little less if you have just browned it and it has not become cold). Leave to rest out of the oven for about 10 minutes. Any juices from the roasting tin can be added to the sauce.

Carve and serve with the sauce and more redcurrant jelly, if you like, accompanied by red cabbage.

AGA COOKING Brown the meat on the boiling plate, then cook in the roasting oven for about 12 minutes.

You'll need 2 large lemon soles to produce the 4 large fillets which are halved and the pieces assembled together with a dill and crab filling, then topped with a cheesy crust. Ensure the crabmeat is very well drained, otherwise the sauce will be wet. If making ahead, allow the sauce to become completely cold before mixing in the crabmeat.

SOLE and CRAB *with a crispy cheese topping*

SERVES 4

- 40g (1½oz) butter, plus more for the dish
- 1 level tablespoon flour
- 150ml (¼ pint) milk
- 2 tablespoons double cream
- 1 egg yolk
- a few drops of Tabasco sauce
- 2 tablespoons chopped fresh dill
- 100g can of fresh white crab meat
- 4 large lemon sole fillets, skinned and halved lengthways

FOR THE TOPPING

- 25g (1oz) white breadcrumbs
- 50g (2oz) mature Cheddar cheese, grated
- a little paprika

You will need a 23 x 30cm (9 x 12 inch) shallow ovenproof dish, buttered.

First make the sauce: melt the butter and blend in the flour. Cook for a few moments, then gradually pour on the milk, stirring briskly, and bring to the boil, stirring. Remove from the heat, stir in the cream and season with salt and pepper. Beat in the egg yolk, Tabasco, dill and well-drained crab meat.

Lay the four larger fillets of sole in the base of the buttered dish. Season with salt and pepper. Spread the crabmeat mixture over the top and lay the remaining four fillets over the top. Season with salt and pepper again.

Mix the breadcrumbs and cheese together for the topping and scatter over the fish, then dust with paprika.

● ***This can be made up to 12 hours ahead and kept covered in the fridge. It is not suitable for freezing.***

Bake in an oven preheated to 200°C/180°C fan/gas 6 for about 20–25 minutes, until bubbling, golden brown and crisp, and the fish is done.

Serve piping hot, with buttered new potatoes.

AGA COOKING Bake on the top set of runners in the roasting oven for about 20 minutes.

fish

This is a really simple but interesting way of serving whole trout, which are still a bargain in the shops. Be sure that the foil is well buttered under the tails of the fish, as the tails are prone to stick during cooking.

baked TROUT with lime and garlic

pictured on pages 88–9

SERVES 4

100g (4oz) soft butter, plus more for the tin
finely grated zest and juice of 2 limes
3 garlic cloves, crushed
4 tablespoons chopped parsley leaves, stalks reserved
4 whole rainbow trout, each about 300g (10oz), cleaned and scaled

Mix together the butter, lime zest, garlic and chopped parsley in a small bowl, then season with salt and pepper.

Make 3 deep slashes on one side of the trout, cutting down as far as the backbone, and push the flavoured butter into each incision. There will be too much, so reserve some for later use in the sauce.

Line a large roasting tin with foil, butter that well and sprinkle with salt and pepper. Arrange the trout in the tin, cut side up.

Squeeze the juice from the limes and reserve. Cut the lime skins into slices and stuff these into the belly of the trout with the parsley stalks.

● ***The trout can now be kept in the fridge for up to 24 hours. They are not suitable for freezing.***

When ready to cook, preheat the oven to 220°C/200°C fan/gas 7. Cook in the preheated oven for about 12–15 minutes. Check along the backbone to see when the fish is done; the flesh will become opaque.

Carefully lift the fish on to a warm serving dish. Tip the roasting tin juices into a small saucepan and add the reserved lime juice. Boil to reduce a little, then whisk in the reserved lime butter until just melted – don't let it boil or it will separate.

Remove the heads from the fish and discard them. Peel the skin and fins from the top side of the fish and discard them. Pour the sauce over the exposed fish flesh. Serve with sautéed courgette wedges.

AGA COOKING Bake on the top set of runners in the roasting oven for about 10–12 minutes.

This kedgeree is perfect to serve for a family supper, or it can easily be doubled for larger numbers. Try to keep the fish nice and chunky, so you can see big pieces in the rice mixture.

smoked HADDOCK kedgeree

SERVES 4–6

1 tablespoon oil
1 onion, roughly chopped
1 teaspoon medium curry powder
1 teaspoon ground turmeric
750g ($1\frac{1}{2}$ lb) undyed smoked haddock fillet, skin on
small bunch of parsley
600ml (1 pint) milk
225g (8oz) easy-cook rice
50g (2oz) butter, plus another optional 50g (2oz) if reheating
juice of 1 lemon
3 hard-boiled eggs, shelled and quartered
mango chutney, to serve

Heat the oil in a pan, add the onion and fry it gently over a low heat for about 15 minutes, until softened. Stir in the curry powder and turmeric, and fry for a few minutes more.

Place the haddock in a large pan, add the crushed parsley stalks (chop the leaves and reserve for garnish) and pour on the milk. Cover with a lid, bring to the boil and simmer for 3 minutes. Set aside, covered, for about 5–10 minutes, until the fish is cooked.

Strain the milk into a measuring jug. You will need 360ml (12fl oz). Pour into a saucepan and add the rice – no salt is required. Bring to the boil and cook for 15–20 minutes, until the rice is tender and the liquid absorbed.

Peel the skin from the cooked haddock and discard it, then break the flesh into large chunks. Remove any bones.

Add the butter to the onion and heat until it is melted. Stir in the rice, fish and the lemon juice. Season with pepper and salt if needed. Mix well and place the egg quarters on top. Sprinkle with the chopped reserved parsley.

● *The kedgeree can be made ahead and cooled, then reheated covered with some buttered foil for about 15 minutes in an oven preheated to 180°C/160°C fan/gas 4 until hot. You may find it a little dry; if so, gently stir in 50g (2oz) butter. The kedgeree also reheats well in the microwave, covered in cling film, as it does not dry out. It is not suitable for freezing.*

Serve with mango chutney.

AGA COOKING Bring the rice to the boil, cover and transfer to the simmering oven for about 15 minutes, until all the liquid has been absorbed. Reheat the cooked kedgeree covered in the roasting oven for 15–20 minutes.

Fish pie is one of my great stand-bys and can be prepared entirely ahead. What makes this one so special is its layers of smoked and fresh haddock, blended with a dill sauce, topped with heaps of mustard cheesy mash. I can be out all day knowing that I have a delicious supper ready for family or friends. Serve the pie with a simple green salad.

exceedingly good double FISH PIE

SERVES 6–8

50g (2 oz) butter, plus more for the dish
350g (12 oz) skinned undyed smoked haddock fillet
350g (12 oz) skinned haddock fillet
2 leeks, sliced
50g (2 oz) flour
600ml (1 pint) hot milk
juice of 1/2 lemon
2 tablespoons fresh chopped dill
3 hard-boiled eggs, shelled and roughly chopped

FOR THE TOPPING

1kg (2 1/4 lb) potatoes, peeled and cut into even-sized pieces
about 150ml (1/4 pint) milk
2 heaped tablespoons grainy mustard
75g (3 oz) mature Cheddar cheese, grated

Butter a 2 litre (3 1/2 pint) shallow pie dish about 6cm (2 1/2 inches) deep.

Cut the fish into 1cm (1/2 inch) pieces, discarding any skin and bones. Boil the leeks in salted water for about 5 minutes and drain well.

Next make the sauce: melt the 50g (2 oz) butter in a good-sized pan, add the flour and cook for a few moments, not allowing it to colour. Whisk in half the hot milk and allow to thicken. Whisk in the remaining hot milk and keep whisking until smooth. Add the fish and a little salt and pepper. Cook over a low heat for 2 minutes, stirring. Add the lemon juice, dill and chopped eggs, and turn out into the buttered dish. Spoon over the leeks and set aside to become completely cold and firm.

Meanwhile, boil the potatoes in salted water until tender, drain and push to one side in the pan. Add the milk and let it become hot, then mash the potatoes with the milk using a potato masher and whisk in the mustard – you may need a little more milk. Check and adjust the seasoning if necessary.

Spread the mash over the cooled fish and scatter with the cheese. Stand the dish in a large roasting tin (just in case it boils over).

● *The pie can be made up to 48 hours ahead. It freezes well without the eggs.*

Bake in an oven preheated to 200°C/180°C fan/gas 6 for about 30 minutes, until the top is golden and the sauce is bubbling at the edges.

VARIATIONS

● Use 500g (1lb 2oz) of lightly cooked spinach instead of the leeks.
● Use all unsmoked haddock and add 200g (7oz) of shelled cooked cold-water prawns instead of the egg.

AGA COOKING Bake on the top set of runners in the roasting oven for about 30 minutes until golden brown and the sauce is bubbling.

This simple dish looks and tastes stunning, and is sure to impress every guest. Choose really fresh sole and get the fishmonger to skin it. You can also make this recipe with plaice fillets.

lemon SOLE with pancetta pockets

SERVES 4

butter for the dish
1 tablespoon olive oil
1 large onion, finely chopped
4 rashers of pancetta or streaky bacon
2 tablespoons chopped fresh parsley
1 teaspoon anchovy sauce
4 large lemon sole fillets, skinned
a little melted butter
a little paprika
4 lemon wedges, to serve

TO FINISH

50g (2oz) butter
juice of 1/2 lemon
1 tablespoon chopped fresh parsley

Butter and season the base of an ovenproof dish big enough to take the sole in a single layer.

Heat the oil in a frying pan, add the onion and cook gently over a low heat for about 15 minutes until tender.

Snip the pancetta into small pieces, add to the onion, increase the heat and fry until crisp. Transfer to a plate and leave to become completely cold, then stir in the parsley, anchovy sauce and black pepper.

Arrange the fillets in the buttered dish, skinned side uppermost. Season the fish and divide the stuffing into four, then spoon in the centre of the fillets. Hold each end of the fillets and twist them in opposite directions to form a pocket showing the stuffing – rather like a straight croissant. Brush the fillets with melted butter and sprinkle with paprika.

● *Cover with cling film and keep in the fridge for up to 12 hours. The fillets are not suitable for freezing.*

Bake in an oven preheated to 180°C/160°C fan/gas 4 for about 12–15 minutes until the fish is cooked and has turned a matt white.

To finish: melt the butter in a saucepan, add the lemon juice and parsley and pour over the sole. Serve at once with the lemon wedges.

AGA COOKING Slide the dish on to the second set of runners in the roasting oven for about 10–15 minutes until the fish is just cooked.

Lightly smoked Scottish salmon fillets are well worth looking out for. They are sometimes sold in packs or individual portions in the better supermarkets and fishmongers. The salmon has been run through a kiln for a short time to give a lightly oak-smoked flavour.

lightly smoked SCOTTISH SALMON *with sautéed cucumber*

SERVES 6

125g tub of full-fat cream cheese
3 tablespoons creamed horseradish
2 tablespoons fresh dill, chopped
6 lightly smoked salmon fillets, skinned, each about 150g (5oz)
50g (2oz) butter, plus more for the baking sheet
6 tablespoons coarse fresh white breadcrumbs
a little paprika
1 medium cucumber
juice of 1 lemon
1–2 tablespoon(s) chopped fresh dill

Spoon the cream cheese into a mixing bowl, stir in the horseradish and dill, and season with salt and pepper.

Season both sides of the salmon with salt and pepper and place, skinned side down, on a buttered baking sheet.

Spread the cheese mixture over the top of the salmon fillets. Press on the breadcrumbs and sprinkle with a little paprika.

● ***The salmon with the crust can be kept covered in the fridge up to 24 hours ahead. It is not suitable for freezing.***

Bake in an oven preheated to 200°C/180°fan/gas 6 for about 9–11 minutes (remember the salmon has been lightly smoked, so will cook more quickly).

Meanwhile, peel the cucumber using a potato peeler and cut it into slices the thickness of medium-sliced bread. Heat the 50g (2oz) butter in a frying pan over a high heat, add the cucumber slices and fry until lightly browned on both sides. Season with salt and pepper, then add the lemon juice and dill.

Immediately arrange the hot cucumber on a large serving dish or individual plates and sit the salmon fillets on top to serve.

AGA COOKING Slide the baking sheet with the salmon on to the second set of runners in the roasting oven for about 9–11 minutes. Fry the cucumber on the boiling plate.

The salmon fillet looks stunning with the red pepper topping and finely shredded basil. If you can't get middle-cut of salmon fillet, you could use tail fillets, as these too give a wide surface for the red pepper topping. Don't shred the basil until the last minute, or it will bruise and go limp.

SALMON with red pepper *and basil chiffonnade*

SERVES 6

3 red peppers
6 middle-cut salmon fillets, each about 150g (5oz), skinned
butter for the baking sheet
6 good teaspoons full-fat cream cheese
6 teaspoons balsamic vinegar
small bunch of basil

Preheat the grill. Cut the peppers in half and remove the core and seeds. Arrange the peppers, cut side down, on the grill pan and grill until charred. Slide the blackened peppers into a plastic bag and seal until cold. Once cold, peel the peppers and slice into thin strips.

Arrange the salmon on a greased baking sheet and season with salt and pepper. Season the cream cheese with salt and pepper, and spread each fillet with a teaspoon of cream cheese, then lay the strips of pepper on top.

● ***This can be made 12 hours ahead, covered and kept in the fridge. It is not suitable for freezing.***

Bake in an oven preheated to 200°C/180°C fan/gas 6 for about 15 minutes until the fish is opaque in the centre. Do not overcook or the salmon will become dry.

Lift on to a warm serving plate and drizzle each fillet with balsamic vinegar. Roll the basil leaves like a cigar and slice that across to shred the basil very finely. Sprinkle the basil chiffonnade over the red peppers and serve at once.

AGA COOKING Cut the peppers in half, brush with oil, arrange on the baking sheet and cook on the top set of runners in the roasting oven for about 15 minutes until charred. Cook the salmon for about 10 minutes on the top set of runners in the roasting oven.

pasta + *rice*

This light pasta dish, a simple blend of spaghetti with garlic, courgettes, pesto and Parmesan cheese, is perfect for non-meat eaters. The tomatoes and basil give a wonderful colour and flavour. It is best served straight away, otherwise the courgettes lose their colour.

pesto SPAGHETTI with courgettes *and parmesan*

SERVES 4–6

- 1 tablespoon olive oil
- 1 large onion, roughly chopped
- 200g (7oz) courgettes
- 350g (12oz) spaghetti
- 2 garlic cloves, crushed
- 3 tablespoons pesto
- 100g (4oz) sun-blushed tomatoes, snipped into small pieces
- 1 large bunch of fresh basil, roughly chopped
- 50g (2oz) Parmesan cheese, grated

Cook the spaghetti in salted boiling water according to the packet instructions or until al dente, then drain.

● *Prepare the ingredients up to 8 hours ahead and cook and serve immediately. The onion can be softened and left in the frying pan up to 4 hours ahead. The pasta can be cooked up to 8 hours ahead (if so, refresh the just-cooked pasta quickly in cold water to stop the cooking process). Not suitable for freezing.*

Heat the oil in a large non-stick-frying pan. Add the onion and cook slowly, covered with a lid, for about 15 minutes or until the onions are soft. Slice the courgettes in half lengthways, remove the seeds with a teaspoon and coarsely grate.

Add the courgettes and garlic to the frying pan and fry over a high heat for about 2 minutes. Then add the pesto and sun-blushed tomatoes, together with the pasta and, if necessary, reheat until piping-hot. Season well.

Add the basil at the last minute, then pour into a warm serving dish to serve. Sprinkle with Parmesan cheese and serve at once.

AGA COOKING Cook on the boiling plate. Soften the onion, covered, in the simmering plate for about 15 minutes until soft.

Another great family supper recipe, this is a variation on the classic Italian puttanesca recipe with added aubergine. The sauce freezes well or can be made ahead and kept in the fridge for up to 3 days.

PENNE puttanesca

SERVES 4

225g (8oz) penne pasta
grated Parmesan cheese, to serve

FOR THE PUTTANESCA SAUCE

3 tablespoons olive oil
1 small aubergine, chopped into small 2cm (1 inch) cubes
1 red chilli, deseeded and finely chopped
3 garlic cloves, crushed
400g tin of chopped tomatoes
50g (2oz) anchovies in oil, drained and finely chopped
100g (4oz) pitted green olives, halved
small bunch of basil, chopped
2 tablespoons chopped parsley

Cook the pasta in boiling salted water according to the packet instructions or until al dente, then drain.

Heat 2 tablespoons of the oil in a large non-stick frying pan, add the aubergine and fry over a high heat for about 5 minutes, until soft and golden brown.

Add the remaining oil, together with the chilli and garlic, and fry for 2 minutes. Add the tomatoes with their liquid, the anchovies and olives. Simmer uncovered for about 5 minutes and season with a little salt and pepper.

● ***The pasta can be cooked up to 8 hours ahead (if so, refresh the just-cooked pasta quickly in cold water to stop the cooking process). The sauce can be made up to 3 days ahead and is suitable for freezing.***

Mix the pasta with the hot pasta sauce in the pan and, if necessary, reheat until piping hot. Check the seasoning and adjust if necessary. Sprinkle with the basil and parsley, and serve with grated Parmesan cheese.

This is remarkably easy to make. If you are eating the lasagne soon after making it, say in 2 hours' time, pre-soak the lasagne sheets in hand-hot water for about 10 minutes before layering, to soften the pasta. If you are making it 12 hours ahead, you could use no-cook dry lasagne.

LASAGNE revisited

SERVES 6

butter for the dish
8 sheets of fresh lasagne
100g (4oz) fresh Parmesan cheese, grated

FOR THE BOLOGNESE SAUCE

1 tablespoon olive oil
500g (1lb) raw lean minced beef
1 large onion, roughly chopped
2 garlic cloves, crushed
2 level tablespoons flour
2 (400g) cans of chopped tomatoes
3 tablespoons tomato purée
1 teaspoon sugar

FOR THE CREME FRAICHE SAUCE

2 tablespoons cornflour
1 tablespoon Dijon mustard
500g tub of low-fat crème fraîche

Butter an oblong dish about 23 x 30cm (9 x 12 inches) and about 6cm (2½ inches) deep.

To make the Bolognese sauce, heat the oil in a large non-stick frying pan and brown the mince all over. Add the onion and garlic, sprinkle in the flour and stir. Stir in the tomatoes, tomato purée and sugar, and season. Bring to the boil, cover and simmer for about an hour, or until tender.

To make the crème fraîche sauce, measure the cornflour into a saucepan, add the mustard and 2 tablespoons of the crème fraîche, then whisk until smooth. Add the remaining crème fraîche and season to taste. Bring to the boil, whisking, until it thickens slightly. Be careful that it doesn't stick on the base.

To layer the lasagne, divide the meat sauce in three and spoon one-third into the base of the prepared dish. Spoon a third of the crème fraîche sauce over the top of that and roughly spread over, then sprinkle with one-third of the Parmesan. Arrange a single layer of 4 sheets of the pasta on top without overlapping. Repeat the layering, using two more layers each of the meat sauce and crème fraîche sauce and one of the pasta, so the final layer is crème fraîche sauce. Sprinkle the remaining Parmesan on top.

● ***This can be made up to 48 hours ahead, covered and kept in the fridge. It also freezes well before cooking.***

Cook in an oven preheated to 220°C/200°C fan/gas 7 for about 25–35 minutes, or until the top is golden brown and the pasta is tender.

Serve with a mixed leaf salad and some good crusty Italian bread.

AGA COOKING Make the Bolognese sauce on the boiling plate. Cover and transfer to the simmering oven for about an hour, until tender. Bake the completed dish on the second set of runners in the roasting oven for about 25 minutes, until golden brown and the pasta is tender.

This is a very simple supper dish, needing only some crisp bread to serve.

pancetta tagliatelle

SERVES 4–6

350g (12 oz) tagliatelle
200g (7 oz) pancetta, chopped into small dice
4 courgettes, chopped into small dice
200ml carton of full-fat crème fraîche
100g (4 oz) Parmesan cheese, grated
4 tablespoons chopped parsley

Cook the pasta in boiling salted water until just al dente, about 10 minutes or according to packet instructions, then drain.

While the pasta is cooking, fry the pancetta in a non-stick frying pan until the fat is beginning to run, then add the courgettes and cook them until golden brown.

● ***The pasta can be cooked up to 8 hours ahead (if so, refresh the just-cooked pasta quickly in cold water to stop the cooking process), and the pancetta and courgettes can be fried up to 4 hours ahead.***

Add the crème fraîche to the courgettes, bring to the boil and season. Add the Parmesan cheese and the cooked tagliatelle, and toss together until piping-hot.

Tip into a warmed bowl and sprinkle with the chopped parsley.

AGA COOKING Cook on the boiling plate of the Aga.

Carrots and celery give the risotto texture and still are crunchy when it is cooked.

herb chicken risotto

SERVES 6

50g (2oz) butter
2 large chicken breasts, skinned and sliced into small thin strips
1 onion, finely chopped
2 carrots, peeled and chopped into small dice
2 celery stalks, diced
350g (12oz) Arborio rice
150ml (1/4 pint) white wine
about 1 litre (1 1/2 pints) good chicken stock
juice of 1 lemon
1 tablespoon chopped thyme leaves
2 tablespoons chopped parsley
75g (3oz) Parmesan cheese, grated

Melt half of the butter in a large deep non-stick frying pan. Brown the chicken strips in this very quickly until just cooked, then transfer to a plate.

Melt the remaining butter in the pan and add the onion, carrots and celery. Fry for 2 minutes, then add the rice and stir to coat the grains of rice in the mixture. Stir in the wine.

Pour the stock into a saucepan and bring to the boil, then simmer. Add ladlefuls of the hot stock to the rice, stirring all of the time, until all the liquid is absorbed and the rice is cooked, this will take about 20 minutes. You may not need all of the stock.

● ***The risotto can be prepared ahead up to this stage, for about 12 hours ahead. It is not suitable for freezing.***

Add the chicken, lemon juice and thyme, and heat though, adding a little more stock if needed. Add the parsley and 50g (2oz) of the Parmesan, spoon into a warmed serving bowl and sprinkle the remaining cheese on top. Serve at once.

AGA COOKING Cook on the simmering plate of the Aga.

This is easy to do, as it is all cooked in one pot, and has a wonderful flavour, so it is perfect for the family.

one-pot chicken and mediterranean rice

SERVES 4

- 4 small boneless, skinless chicken breasts
- a little paprika
- 2 tablespoons oil
- 1 large onion, chopped
- 70g pancetta, snipped into small pieces
- 2cm (1 inch) fresh ginger, peeled and grated
- 1 small red chilli, finely chopped
- 225g (8oz) long-grain rice
- 450ml (3/4 pint) chicken stock
- 50g (2oz) black olives, pitted and halved
- 2 tablespoons stripped fresh thyme leaves

Season the chicken breasts with salt and pepper, and sprinkle a little paprika over each. Heat 1 tablespoon of the oil in a large, deep frying pan or casserole and brown the chicken breasts for a few minutes on each side until golden brown. Transfer to a plate and set aside.

Add the remaining oil to the pan, then add the onion, pancetta, ginger, chilli and 1/2 teaspoon of paprika. Fry for a few minutes over a high heat.

Add the rice and stock, bring to the boil, then add the chicken, cover and simmer for about 15 minutes until the rice and chicken are cooked.

● *This can be made completely to this stage up to 12 hours ahead; reheat gently, adding a little more stock if needed. It is not suitable for freezing.*

Stir in the olives and thyme, and serve hot.

AGA COOKING Brown the chicken on the boiling plate and continue making the recipe in a large frying pan. Bring to the boil, cover and transfer to the simmering oven for about 15–20 minutes, until the rice is tender and chicken is cooked through.

vegetable *side dishes*

This is a wonderful alternative to potato salad. Peel the celeriac with a small sharp knife, not with a vegetable peeler – otherwise it takes too long! This salad is excellent with cold meats, like the Parma ham shown here.

spicy mustard CELERIAC salad

SERVES 4–8

1 medium celeriac root
2 teaspoons Dijon mustard
6 tablespoons mayonnaise
juice of 1 lemon

Using a large sharp knife, cut the celeriac into quarters. Carefully peel off the skin thickly, using a small sharp knife. Coarsely grate the celeriac, either by hand or in a processor.

Blanch the shreds in boiling salted water for about 1 minute, drain in a colander and refresh under cold water to stop them cooking. Drain well.

● ***The blanched grated celeriac can be kept covered in the fridge for up to 12 hours. Dress just before serving.***

Mix the remaining ingredients together in a large salad bowl and season with salt and pepper.

Tip the blanched celeriac into the dressing in the salad bowl and toss together to serve.

This salad looks stunning as the colours are vibrant. If you have friends or family with a nut allergy, just omit the walnuts. If you don't have a julienne blade for your food processor, very coarsely grate the beetroot and carrot instead.

julienne beetroot and carrot salad

SERVES 4–8

5 medium raw beetroot, peeled
2 medium carrots, peeled
50g (2 oz) shelled walnuts, coarsely chopped if you like

FOR THE MUSTARD DRESSING

1 tablespoon grainy mustard
2 tablespoons white wine vinegar
2 tablespoons runny honey
4 tablespoons olive oil

Fit a food processor with its julienne blade. Process the beetroot and carrots until in fine julienne (like matchsticks).

Arrange these in a salad bowl and season with salt and pepper.

● *The beetroot and carrot can be cut into julienne strips up to 24 hours ahead, then kept covered in the fridge. Dress the salad at the last minute. It is not suitable for freezing.*

Make the dressing by putting the ingredients into a clean jam jar, screw on the lid and shake until combined. Pour over the beetroot and carrot. Toss in the walnuts.

This salad looks stunning and tastes delicious. Nuts keep well in the freezer and defrost in seconds; freezing prevents them from going rancid.

watermelon, FETA and pine nut salad

SERVES 6

2 bags of lambs' lettuce or rocket
1/2 small watermelon
200g (7 oz) good-quality feta cheese
50g (2 oz) pine nuts, toasted as described on page 118

FOR THE DRESSING

juice of 1 lime
6 tablespoons olive oil
3 teaspoons honey
2 teaspoons white wine vinegar

Scatter the lambs' lettuce over a large flat serving platter. Cut the watermelon into about 6 wedges, remove the seeds using a teaspoon and remove the skin with a sharp knife. Slice into large thick triangles and arrange over the top of the lettuce. Crumble over the feta and sprinkle over the toasted pine nuts.

Make the dressing by measuring the ingredients into a jar. Season with salt and pepper and shake well.

● ***The salad ingredients can be prepared up to 12 hours ahead and kept separately in the fridge. The dressing can be made up to a week ahead.***

Pour the dressing over the salad and serve.

These are perfect to accompany any barbecued meat, poultry or fish. If just having these kebabs on their own, serve with a dip such as diced cucumber in yoghurt.

VEGETABLE kebabs

SERVES 6

1 large red pepper
12 fat asparagus spears, cut into three widthways
12 small chestnut mushrooms
12 small picking onions, peeled and halved
a little olive oil

You will need 6 skewers.

Cut the pepper in half, remove the seeds and cut each half into 12 pieces.

Thread a piece of pepper, a piece of asparagus, a mushroom and an onion on to each skewer and repeat again. Continue using up all the vegetables.

● ***These can be made ahead and kept in the fridge. Cook just before serving. They are not suitable for freezing.***

Cover a baking sheet with piece of foil and arrange the kebabs on top. Brush the kebabs with a little oil and season well. Bake in an oven preheated to 200°C/180°C fan/gas 6 for about 10–15 minutes until soft.

Serve hot.

Red cabbage must be one of the best of the winter vegetables. It is delicious with game, especially the Peppered venison on page 84, but is just as good with the humble sausage. It is very difficult to overcook red cabbage, so don't worry if it is in the oven a bit longer than I suggest.

gingered RED cabbage

SERVES 8

40g ($1^1/_2$ oz) butter
1 medium red cabbage, sliced
1 large onion, roughly chopped
2 tablespoons freshly grated ginger
2–3 good tablespoons redcurrant jelly

Preheat the oven 165°C/145°C fan/gas 3.

Melt the butter in a large pan, cover with half the red cabbage and season with salt and pepper. Add the onion, ginger and the remaining cabbage. Stir over a high heat for about 5 minutes.

Cover and transfer to the preheated oven for about $1^1/_2$ hours, stirring from time to time, until very tender. Stir in the redcurrant jelly and check and adjust the seasoning if necessary.

● ***This can be made up to 48 hours ahead and reheated in a low oven to serve. It also freezes well once cooked.***

Serve hot.

AGA COOKING Heat on the boiling plate, stir as above for about 5 minutes, cover, transfer to the simmering oven for about 2 hours until tender.

This is a lovely way of serving winter veg – you can use any combination. Cut them the same size, so they roast at the same rate. To toast the pine nuts, dry-fry them in a non-stick pan over a medium heat, turning them all the time, until just pale golden.

double-roasted winter vegetables *with pine nuts*

SERVES 4–6

550g (1lb 4oz) butternut squash,
500g (1lb 2oz) parsnips, peeled
2 tablespoons vegetable oil
50g (2oz) pine nuts, toasted (see above)

Preheat the oven to 200°C/180C°fan/gas 6.

Cut the squash in half lengthways and remove the seeds. Peel the squash, using a small sharp knife, and cut into 2cm (1-inch) cubes. Cut the parsnip into 2cm (1-inch) cubes.

Put both vegetables into a large roasting tin, season with salt and pepper and toss in the oil, using your hands.

Roast in the preheated oven for about 30 minutes until tender, crisp and golden brown, tossing halfway through. Season lightly and scatter over the pine nuts.

● *On the morning of serving, or the day before, roast for about 15 minutes, then keep in a cool place until needed. To serve, roast again for about 20 minutes and sprinkle over the pine nuts just before serving. Not suitable for freezing.*

AGA COOKING Roast on the floor of the roasting oven for about 30 minutes until tender, crisp and golden brown, tossing halfway through.

This wonderful modern stuffing is crisp and full of flavour. The butternut squash is in large pieces, clearly seen. There is no need to toast the pine nuts as they are roasted with the stuffing. This is best served with roast turkey, chicken or pork, and is also ideal as a dish on its own for vegetarians, serving 3–4.

butternut squash and pine nut stuffing

SERVES 4–6

50g (2oz) butter, cut into small pieces, plus more for the dish
1 large onion, roughly chopped
3 celery stalks, strings removed and roughly chopped
1 large butternut squash
1 tablespoon vegetable oil
225g (8oz) breadcrumbs
100g (4oz) pine nuts
grated zest of 1 lemon
3 heaped tablespoons chopped parsley
2 tablespoons chopped rosemary

First generously butter a 23cm x 32cm (9 x 13 inches) ovenproof dish.

Place the onion and celery in a saucepan, cover with cold water, bring to the boil and simmer for about 5 minutes, until the vegetables are almost tender. Drain well and stir in the pieces of butter.

Peel the butternut squash, remove the seeds and cut into 2cm (1 inch) pieces. Fry or roast the butternut squash in the oil until just lightly browned but not cooked. Mix this and all the remaining ingredients together with the onion and celery, and season. Spoon into the well-buttered dish without smoothing the top.

● ***This can be made to this point up to 24 hours ahead and then cooked to serve. It is not suitable for freezing.***

Bake in an oven preheated to 220°C/200°C fan/gas 7 for about 25–30 minutes, until the surface is crisp and the squash is tender.

AGA COOKING Roast the completed dish on the second set of runners in the roasting oven for about 25–30 minutes, until the surface is crisp and the squash is tender.

I adore this recipe, which I serve with meat or fish, but could just as well eat as it is. It is essential to pre-cook the potatoes and fennel, otherwise they absorb too much butter and you would have to use more, giving an over-rich result.

FENNEL and potato gratin

pictured on pages 120–21

SERVES 4–6

- 50g (2 oz) butter, plus more for the dish
- 3 large fennel bulbs
- 600g (1 lb 6oz) large potatoes, peeled
- 2 garlic cloves, crushed
- 50g (2 oz) Parmesan cheese, grated

Butter a shallow 2.4 litre (4 pint) ovenproof dish about 23 x 30 cm (9 x 12 inches).

Trim the tops from the fennel and cut each bulb in half through the root, then cut each half lengthways into 3 wedges.

Cut the potatoes into wedges the same size as the fennel wedges.

Boil the fennel in a large pan of salted water for about 5 minutes, then add the potatoes and boil for a further 5 minutes, until both vegetables are just tender. Drain and dry well, then arrange in the buttered dish. Season well with salt and pepper.

Put the 50g butter and the garlic in a small pan and set over a low heat until just melted. Pour over the fennel and potato in the dish. Sprinkle with the Parmesan.

● **This can be prepared and assembled in the dish up to 12 hours ahead. It is not suitable for freezing.**

Slide into an oven preheated to 200°C/180°fan/gas 6 for about 30–40 minutes, until piping hot and golden brown.

AGA COOKING Slide on to the top set of runners in the roasting oven for about 30–40 minutes, until piping hot, golden brown and tender.

Rösti potatoes make a great supper dish, topped with fried eggs and bacon.

rösti potatoes

SERVES 4

750g (1½lb) roasting potatoes, peeled
½ small onion
50g (2oz) butter, melted
3 tablespoons olive oil

Coarsely grate the potatoes and onion (this can be easily done in a processor) and put into a clean tea towel, then wring out as much moisture as possible before placing in a bowl.

Stir the melted butter into the potato and onion in the bowl, season with salt and pepper, and mix well.

Heat the olive oil in a 20cm (8-inch) non-stick frying pan. Add the potato and onion mixture and press down. Cook over a high heat until the underside is golden brown, about 3–5 minutes, shaking the pan from time to time.

Using a non-stick fish slice, carefully turn the rösti over and continue to cook for a further 8–10 minutes until the other side is golden brown and cooked through.

● ***The cooked rösti can be made up to 12 hours ahead and reheated in a hot (220°C/200°C fan/gas 7) oven for about 10 minutes.***

Tip on to a plate, cut into wedges and serve hot.

AGA COOKING Cook on the boiling plate. After flipping over, transfer to floor of the roasting oven for about 15 minutes until the underside is brown and the potatoes are tender.

This is perfect for non-meat eaters or to serve with other curries. It is also nice on its own, served with extra mango chutney and poppadoms.

mild aubergine and LENTIL curry

with a hint of cardamom

SERVES 4–6

- 1 tablespoon olive oil
- 1 large onion, roughly chopped
- 2 cm (1-inch) piece of fresh ginger, peeled and finely grated
- 1 small aubergine, cut into small cubes
- 6 cardamom pods
- 1½ tablespoons medium curry powder
- ½ teaspoon ground turmeric
- 2 (410g) tins of cooked lentils, drained
- 300 ml (½ pint) vegetable stock
- 2 tablespoons mango chutney
- 200g tub of Greek yoghurt
- juice of ½–1 lemon, to taste
- 2 tablespoons chopped parsley

Heat the oil in large non-stick frying pan. Add the onion and fry over a high heat for a minute. Lower the heat, cover and simmer for about 10 minutes, until beginning to soften.

Add the ginger and aubergine, and fry until turning golden brown. Remove the husks from the cardamom pods and bash the seeds until fine. Sprinkle over the vegetables, with the curry powder and turmeric, and fry for a minute.

Stir in the lentils and blend in the stock, mango chutney and yoghurt. Season with salt and pepper. Cover and simmer over a low heat for about 15–20 minutes, until the onions and aubergine are tender. Stir in lemon juice to taste.

● *This can be made up to 24 hours ahead. It is not suitable for freezing.*

Serve piping hot, sprinkled with chopped parsley

AGA COOKING Fry the onion on the boiling plate for a couple of minutes, cover and transfer to the simmering oven for about 10 minutes to soften. Continue as above and return to the simmering oven for about 20 minutes, until the onions and aubergine are tender.

This is perfect to eat on its own, perhaps with a green salad, or to accompany steaks, and, being baked in one dish, makes an easy family supper. Replace the bacon with ham if some needs using up. If time is short, don't bother peeling the potatoes. Reblochon is one of France's great mountain cheeses, from the Haute-Savoie region. Taleggio is a soft cows'-milk cheese from northern Italy with a distinctive flavour.

tartiflette

SERVES 4-6

butter for the dish

800g (1³/4 lb) small new potatoes, such as Charlotte

1–2 tablespoons olive oil

1 large onion, finely chopped

250g (9 oz) streaky smoked bacon, chopped

250g (9 oz) button mushrooms, halved

150g (5 oz) Reblochon or Taleggio cheese, rind removed

150ml (1/4 pint) pouring double cream

a little paprika

2 tablespoons chopped fresh parsley

Butter an ovenproof dish about 18 x 25cm (7½ x 10 inches).

Boil the potatoes in salted water until tender. Drain and, when cool enough to handle but still warm, slice thickly. Arrange in the buttered dish.

Heat the oil in a large frying pan, add the onion and fry for a few minutes over a high heat. Add the bacon and fry for a few minutes, then lower the heat, cover and cook for about 20 minutes, until tender, stirring occasionally.

Add the mushrooms to the pan and fry over a high heat for 3 minutes. Scatter over the potatoes and stir in. Coarsely grate the cheese over the potato mixture.

● ***This can be prepared to this stage up to 12 hours ahead and kept in the fridge. If cooking straight from the fridge, it will take a little longer in the oven. It is not suitable for freezing.***

Preheat the oven to 200°C/180°C fan/gas 6. Pour the seasoned cream over the top of the potato mixture, sprinkle with paprika and bake in preheated oven for about 15 minutes until crisp on top and piping hot. Sprinkle with parsley and serve hot.

AGA COOKING Cook the bacon and onion, covered, in the simmering oven for about 20 minutes until tender. Bake the completed dish on the second set of runners in the roasting oven.

last *courses*

This is a really smart cheat, but is totally delicious. If making it for children, replace the cassis with the same quantity of Ribena. If you don't have any cassis in the cupboard, use vodka or kirsch – the colour will be paler and the flavour a little sharper. As the fruit is frozen and there is plenty of it, it stays suspended in the glass.

summer fruit JELLY

SERVES 6

135g packet of blackcurrant or raspberry flavour jelly
100g (4oz) caster sugar
300ml boiling water
2 tablespoons cassis (blackcurrant liqueur)
380g packet of frozen summer fruits

Break the jelly pieces into a jug, add the sugar and pour over the boiling water. Stir until the jelly and sugar have dissolved.

Stir in the cassis and add enough cold water to make up to 600ml (1 pint).

Divide the frozen fruit between 6 wine glasses. Pour over the jelly mixture.

Transfer to the fridge to set.

● *This can be made completely up to 48 hours ahead. It is not suitable for freezing.*

This looks stunning – all vibrant orange in colour. Other flowers to use for decoration could be petals from an orange coral rose, such as Just Joey or Rosemary Harkness.

ORANGE fruit salad *with flower petals*

SERVES 4–6

- 1 Cantaloupe melon
- 1 mango
- 3 oranges
- 2 tablespoons orange liqueur, such as Grand Marnier or Cointreau
- petals of marigold or a few nasturtium flowers, to decorate

Cut the melon in half and remove the pips. Then slice it into quarters, remove the skin and cut thin slices lengthways, then cut these in half.

Peel the mango, remove the flesh from either side of the stone and slice into thin strips.

Segment the oranges and squeeze the juice from the skin into a fruit bowl. Toss all the fruit in the orange juice and chosen liqueur.

● ***The fruit salad can be made up to 12 hours ahead, covered in cling film and kept in the fridge before serving. It is not suitable for freezing.***

Sprinkle with the flower petals and serve.

This luxurious dessert, which can be made with raspberries or blackberries instead of blueberries if you prefer, is very quick and easy to make, requiring only a few ingredients.

BLUEBERRY and lemon passion

SERVES 4–6

150g (5 oz) fresh blueberries
200ml tub of half-fat crème fraîche
150ml ($^1/_4$ pint) thick Greek-style yoghurt
3 good tablespoons luxury lemon curd
grated zest of 1 lemon and juice of $^1/_2$
icing sugar

You will need 4 wine glasses or 6 shot glasses.

Reserving 3 blueberries for the top of each glass, sprinkle the remaining blueberries in the bottom of each glass.

Stir the crème fraîche, yoghurt and lemon curd together, adding the lemon zest and juice. Taste the cream and, if you think it needs to be a little sharper, add more lemon juice.

Spoon the lemon mixture over the blueberries and smooth the tops. Chill for at least an hour or overnight.

● ***This can be made completely up to 48 hours ahead, then just top with the reserved blueberries and dust with icing sugar before serving. It is not suitable for freezing.***

Decorate each glass with 3 blueberries and dust with icing sugar.

These are basically crème brûlées, but with a lemon passion fruit glaze instead of the brûlée topping. You can also make this mixture in one 900ml (1½-pint) large shallow dish, which will take 30–40 minutes to cook. Here we have made an attractive platter by serving the creams and salad with thin slices of Chocolate Marquise (page 142).

french VANILLA creams *with mango salad*

SERVES 4–6

4 egg yolks
25g (1oz) caster sugar
1 teaspoon vanilla extract
600ml (1 pint) single cream

FOR THE LEMON PASSION GLAZE

1 large passion fruit
2–3 tablespoons luxury lemon curd

TO SERVE

1 large mango
1 passion fruit

Preheat the oven to 160°C/140°C fan/gas 4. You will need 12 very small ramekins (size 3) or 6 larger (size 1) ramekins.

Whisk the egg yolks, sugar and vanilla together in a bowl until combined.

Measure the single cream into a saucepan and heat over a low heat until hand-hot. Pour the hot cream on to the egg mixture and whisk by hand until smooth.

Tip into a jug (to make pouring easier) and pour into the ramekins. Arrange in a roasting tin and pour boiling water to come halfway up the sides of the ramekins.

Bake in the preheated oven for about 15 minutes for the small ones and 25 minutes for the larger, until almost set but still with a wobbly centre. Leave to cool in the roasting tin.

Remove from the tin and chill in the fridge until firm.

● ***These vanilla creams can be made up to 24 hours ahead. They are not suitable for freezing.***

To make the lemon passion topping, scoop out the seeds from the passion fruit and mix together with the lemon curd. Spoon over the cold set vanilla creams (in their ramekins) and chill until needed.

To serve, dice the mango into tiny pieces, about the size of raisins and mix with the pips from the other passion fruit.

Arrange the ramekins on a plate and serve a little mango and passion fruit mixture alongside.

AGA COOKING Slide on to the lower set of runners in the roasting oven for about 8 minutes. Transfer to the simmering oven for a further 45 minutes until just set.

This is a soufflé that can be prepared ahead and cooked to serve. It is very quick to make, quick to cook and just amazing to eat!

divine RASPBERRY soufflé

pictured on page 136-7

SERVES 4–6

butter for the ramekins
300g (10oz) frozen raspberries
1 heaped tablespoon cornflour
3 tablespoons Crème de Framboise or sloe gin
3 egg whites
100g (4oz) caster sugar
a little icing sugar

Butter the insides of 6 (size 1) ramekins.

Measure the raspberries into a saucepan and gently heat to thaw them, bring to simmering point.

Slake the cornflour in the Crème de Framboise in a small bowl or cup, pour into the raspberries and stir briskly. Simmer for about 1–2 minutes. Sieve the mixture, pushing through as much of the raspberry as possible. Set aside to cool.

Whisk the egg whites with an electric whisk on maximum speed until stiff. Still whisking on maximum speed, slowly add the caster sugar, a teaspoonful at a time, until the mixture is stiff and glossy.

Fold the raspberry purée into the egg whites and carefully fold until smooth (being careful not to knock the air out of the egg whites). Spoon into the prepared ramekins and level the top.

● ***The completed soufflés can be made to this stage up to 2 hours ahead and kept in the fridge, then cooked and served immediately. They are not suitable for freezing.***

Preheat the oven to 190°C/170°C fan/gas 5 and preheat a baking sheet to get very hot.

Run your finger around the inside rim of the ramekin (this helps the soufflé to rise evenly). Sit the ramekins on the hot baking sheet and cook for about 8–10 minutes, until well risen.

Dust with icing sugar and serve at once.

AGA COOKING Preheat a baking sheet in the roasting oven to get very hot. Sit the ramekins on top of the baking sheet and slide onto the grid shelf on the floor of the roasting oven for about 8 minutes until well risen.

If you are in a hurry and haven't time to infuse the wine, lemon and sugar overnight, warm the ingredients gently in a pan, just enough to dissolve the sugar, strain and cool, then whisk with the cream.

LEMON syllabub

SERVES 6

small wine glass (100 ml) of sweet white wine
1 lemon
75g (3 oz) caster sugar
300 ml (1/2 pint) double cream
rosemary sprigs, to decorate (optional)

Thinly peel the lemon and squeeze out the juice. Put the wine, lemon juice and rind, and the sugar in a jug, leave to infuse overnight then strain into a bowl.

Pour the cream into the same bowl and whisk until thick and just holding its shape.

Pour into martini glasses or small pots

● ***This can be made up to 48 hours ahead. It is not suitable for freezing.***

Serve chilled, decorate with rosemary sprigs if you like.

This is a good way to turn broken meringues into a smart pudding. Serve with a raspberry coulis or summer berries. Although we normally make this in a loaf tin, if you prefer you can make it in a plastic container and spoon balls of it on to a plate.

lemon MERINGUE ice cream

SERVES 6

50g (2oz) meringues (they can be broken ones)
300ml (1/2 pint) double cream
grated zest and juice of 1 lemon
1/2 jar of homemade or luxury lemon curd
seasonal fruits, to serve

Line a 1lb (450g) loaf tin with cling film.

Lightly break up the meringue into chunky pieces. Whisk the cream lightly until the whisk leaves a trail when lifted. Add the lemon zest and juice, and the lemon curd to the cream. Lastly fold in the meringue, trying not to over-crush the meringue pieces.

Spoon the lemon meringue mixture into the loaf tin and cover with cling film, then freeze for at least 6 hours.

● *The ice cream can be made and kept in the freezer for up to a month.*

If the ice cream has been in the freezer overnight or longer it has to be brought to room temperature for about 10–15 minutes before turning it out on to a plate. Dip a sharp knife in boiling water before slicing it.

Individual slices of the ice cream can be frozen again on a plastic tray and wrapped in cling film if you don't want to serve it all at once.

Serve with seasonal fruits.

This recipe is perfect for serving larger numbers. If making it ahead, use a small pineapple for the ice cream and serve with slices of fresh pineapple on the day.

fresh pineapple ICE CREAM

SERVES 6

1 large fresh pineapple
50g (2oz) icing sugar
juice of 1 small lemon
4 eggs, separated
100g (4oz) caster sugar
300ml (1/2 pint) double cream

Cut the pineapple in half, remove the core and skin, and cut the half into chunks. Whiz the chunks in the processor until smooth. Add the icing sugar and lemon juice, and whiz again.

Cut the remaining pineapple in thin slices ready to serve with the ice cream.

Whisk the egg whites until stiff in a large bowl with an electric hand-whisk or in a free-standing mixer. Once the egg whites look like clouds, gradually add the sugar, still whisking on maximum speed, until stiff and glossy.

In a separate bowl, whisk the cream until it forms soft peaks and fold into the meringue mixture. Stir in the egg yolks and pineapple purée.

Pour into a plastic container and freeze until needed.

● *This can be kept in the freezer for up to 2 months.*

To serve, remove from the freezer 10 minutes before scooping. Arrange 2 scoops of ice cream and about 6 slices of pineapple on each plate. Refreeze any ice cream left over quickly for another day.

As this very rich pudding is perfect for any special occasion it is wonderful to have at the ready in the freezer – you can slice it to serve straight from there. To make strong coffee, dissolve 1 teaspoon of instant coffee in 1 tablespoon of boiling water.

CHOCOLATE marquise

SERVES 8 (gives 16–20 thin slices, 2 slices each)

- 200g (7 oz) Bournville chocolate or similar
- 3 egg yolks
- 75g (3 oz) caster sugar
- 75g (3 oz) soft butter
- 2 tablespoon cocoa powder
- 1 tablespoon strong coffee
- 3 tablespoons brandy
- 150ml (1/4 pint) double cream, lightly whisked
- fresh red berries and pouring cream, to serve

Line a 500g (1 lb) loaf tin with cling film.

Break the chocolate into small pieces and place in a bowl. Sit the bowl over a pan of hot water and stir until completely melted.

Whisk the egg yolks with half the sugar until light, pale and fluffy. Using the same whisk in a separate bowl, beat the butter and remaining sugar until light and fluffy, then beat in the cocoa powder.

Pour the melted chocolate into the cocoa butter mixture, stir in the egg yolk mixture, coffee and brandy, and carefully fold in the cream. Pour the mixture into the prepared loaf tin and cover the top with cling film. Chill for 6–8 hours or overnight.

● ***This can be made up to this point up to 24 hours ahead. It also freezes well.***

It needs to be very cold to slice easily, so freeze for at least 1 hour before slicing. Turn out and remove the cling film. Dip a knife into boiling water, then cut into thin slices and arrange on a plate. Serve chilled with fresh red berries and pouring cream.

These are little shot glasses or small pots of a rich chocolate confection. We find Bournville is the best dark chocolate to use as it is pretty foolproof. For a variation, add a little grated orange zest.

chocolate POTS

SERVES 6

300ml (1/2 pint) single cream
200g (7 oz) plain dark chocolate
2 tablespoons brandy

Reserving 5 tablespoons of the cream in a small jug, put the remaining cream and the chocolate into a small bowl. Sit the bowl over a pan of simmering water and gently heat until the chocolate has just melted into the cream. Stir the chocolate and cream together until blended. Stir in the brandy.

Pour into 6 shot glasses or coffee cups and transfer to the fridge to set for an hour or so.

● **These can be made up to 48 hours ahead and kept in the fridge. They are not suitable for freezing.**

Just before serving, pour over the remaining cream so there is about 1 cm (1/2 inch) of cream floating on the top.

This is an old favourite brought up to date. It is very rich, so serve very thin slices – they can always come back for more!

chocolate tiffin

SERVES 8–10

200g (7 oz) plain chocolate
200g (7 oz) butter, cut into small pieces
2 eggs
25g (1 oz) caster sugar
200g (7 oz) Nice biscuits or similar crumbly biscuits
raspberry coulis and crème fraîche, to serve

You will need a 450g (1 lb) loaf tin lined with foil.

Break the chocolate into small pieces. Slowly melt the chocolate and butter together in a bowl set over a pan of very hot water (but not touching the water) until smooth and runny. Allow to cool.

Whisk the eggs and sugar by hand so they are mixed together, then gradually add the cooled chocolate mixture a little at a time.

Break the biscuits into 1.5cm (1/2-inch) pieces and stir into the mixture. Pour the mixture into the tin and level the top. Leave to set in the fridge for about 6 hours or until firm.

● ***This can be made up to 2 days ahead and kept in the fridge. It freezes well.***

Remove the foil and slice into thin slices. Serve with a raspberry coulis and crème fraîche.

Lucy, my assistant adores this recipe and so we have tested it time and time again! Serve it as a dessert cake, as a pudding or for tea with a fork.

lemon FUDGE cake

SERVES 6–8 (or more, as it is very rich!)

FOR THE BASE

7 plain digestive biscuits, crushed
50g (2oz) butter, melted
25g (1oz) demerara sugar

FOR THE FILLING

2 eggs
150g (5oz) caster sugar
300ml (1/2 pint) double cream
50g (2oz) plain flour
grated zest and juice of 2 lemons

FOR THE TOPPING

150g (5oz) Greek-style yoghurt
2 tablespoons lemon curd

TO DECORATE

100g (4oz) blueberries

Preheat the oven to 180°C/160°C fan/gas 4. Line the base of a 20cm (8-inch) round springform tin with baking parchment.

In a bowl, mix the crushed biscuits with the melted butter and sugar. Stir until all the biscuit is coated and press into the base of the prepared tin.

Make the filling: whisk the eggs and sugar together until blended. Pour in the cream, sift in the flour and whisk until blended. Stir in the lemon juice and zest, and whisk again until combined.

Pour this into the tin on top of biscuit base and bake in the preheated oven for about 35–40 minutes, until the filling has set and is pale golden brown on top.

Remove from the oven and allow to cool in the tin.

● ***This can be made and baked up to 3 days ahead, but ice it on the day of serving. It also freezes well un-iced.***

Mix the topping ingredients together and spread over the cold cake. Decorate with the blueberries.

AGA COOKING Slide the tin on to the lowest set of runners in the roasting oven, with a cold sheet on the second set of runners for about 30 minutes until forming a crust on top. Transfer the hot cold sheet into the simmering oven, sit the cake on top and bake for a further 20–30 minutes until just set.

This consists of a very thin crisp orange shortbread topped with mascarpone and a wealth of summer soft fruits. You can vary the fruit according to the season. Lightly poached apricots on top are excellent in late summer, brushed with apricot jam and sprinkled with toasted almonds.

midsummer open FRUIT tart

SERVES 8

FOR THE ORANGE SHORTBREAD

165g (5½ oz) plain flour
90g (3½ oz) butter, softened
25g (1 oz) icing sugar
grated zest of 1 orange

FOR THE TOPPING

250g tub of mascarpone cheese
5 tablespoons double cream
1 tablespoon caster sugar
a few drops of vanilla extract
400g (11 oz) strawberries
150g (5 oz) raspberries
150g (5 oz) blueberries

FOR THE GLAZE

3–4 tablespoons redcurrant jelly

Preheat the oven to 180°C/160°C fan/gas 4.

Measure the shortbread ingredients into a food processor and whiz until the mix forms into a ball.

Roll the shortbread mix on to non-stick paper or a floured flat baking sheet to make a round about 25cm (10 inches) in diameter.

Using your thumb and index finger, pinch the pastry all the way around the outside to form a crimped edge.

Bake in the preheated oven for about 20–25 minutes until pale golden.

● ***Make and bake the shortbread base up to a week ahead, wrap in foil, then finish the tart on the day. The shortbread base freezes well.***

For the topping, beat the mascarpone, cream, sugar and vanilla together in a bowl until blended.

Take a plate large enough for the shortbread.. Spoon a few blobs of cream mixture onto the plate and sit the shortbread on top (this prevents it from moving). Spread the remaining cream mixture over the shortbread base, leaving a 4cm (1 ½ inch) gap around the edge, so you can see the crimped edge.

Cut the strawberries in half and arrange the halves cut side down on top of the cream. Sprinkle raspberries and blueberries over the strawberries to fill in the gaps.

Gently heat the redcurrant jelly for the glaze and brush it over the fruit.

Serve at room temperature.

AGA COOKING Bake on the grid shelf on the floor of the roasting oven, with the cold sheet on the second set of runners, for about 10 minutes until a pale straw colour. Transfer to the simmering oven to finish, for about 20 minutes.

Apricots also work well in this first-rate Sunday lunch pudding, although their season is shorter. Apples or pears would be delicious too.

hot PLUM torte

SERVES 6–8

75g (3oz) soft butter, plus more for the tin
75g (3oz) caster sugar
100g (4oz) self-raising flour
1 teaspoon baking powder
2 large eggs
finely grated zest of 1 orange
900g (2lb) ripe plums, cut in half, stones removed
about 150g (5oz) demerara sugar
icing sugar, for dusting
cream, ice cream or classic custard, to serve

Generously butter a 28cm (11 inch) ovenproof dish or deep loose-bottomed flan tin about 4cm ($1^1/_2$ inches) deep.

Measure the first six ingredients into a large bowl and beat until smooth.

Spread this mixture evenly over the bottom of the tin or dish. Arrange the plums on top, cut side up, and sprinkle with the demerara sugar to form a thick layer.

● ***The torte can be made completely to this point and kept uncooked in the fridge for up to 12 hours. It is not suitable for freezing.***

When ready to cook, preheat the oven to 200°C/180°C fan/gas 6. Bake the torte in the preheated oven for about 30 minutes, until golden brown and the sponge springs back when pressed.

Serve it from the ovenproof dish if that is how you have made it or, if using a flan tin, loosen the edges of the flan tin with a small palette knife and lift the torte out, leaving it on the base, then carefully slip it on to a serving plate.

Serve warm, dusted with icing sugar and accompanied by cream, ice cream or classic custard.

AGA COOKING 2-oven Aga: Bake on grid shelf on the floor of the roasting oven for about 30 minutes until the cake springs back and is golden brown. If getting too brown, slide the cold sheet on the second set of runners.
3- or 4-oven Aga: Bake on the floor of the baking oven for about 30 minutes until the cake springs back and is golden brown.

This is yet another new version of mince pie, and is so much quicker to make. It looks impressive too.

mincemeat and APPLE galette

SERVES 6–8

FOR THE SHORTBREAD CRUST

175g (6oz) plain flour
110g (4½ oz) butter
60g (2½ oz) icing sugar
grated zest of 1 orange

FOR THE TOPPING

225g (8oz) marzipan, coarsely grated
410g jar of good mincemeat
about 2 red skinned dessert apples, thinly sliced

Preheat the oven to 180°C/160°Cfan/gas 4.

Measure the shortbread crust ingredients a food the processor and whiz until the mixture comes together (do not add any liquid).

Roll the pastry out on a floured flat baking sheet to form a round about 25cm (10 inches) in diameter. Using your thumb and index finger, pinch the pastry all the way around the outside to form a crimped edge.

Mix half the grated marzipan with the mincemeat and spread over the shortbread circle, leaving a 1cm (½ inch) gap around the edge. Arrange the apples in an overlapping spiral over the mincemeat and sprinkle with the remaining marzipan.

Bake in the preheated oven for about 25–30 minutes, until the shortbread is pale golden brown and crisp at the edges.

● ***Cook completely up to 24 hours ahead and reheat in a moderate oven until warm.***

Cut into wedges and serve warm.

AGA COOKING Slide the baking sheet on to the floor of the grid shelf on the floor of the roasting oven, with the cold sheet on the second set of runners, for about 10 minutes, until pale straw colour. Transfer to the simmering oven until cooked through, about 20 minutes.

This makes a wonderful summer dessert, but is perfect for any occasion. Don't worry if the pavlova cracks on the top – this is all part of its charm. Make sure that the hazelnuts are fairly coarsely chopped, as this gives a good texture to the pavlova.

hazelnut pavlova *with mango and passion fruit*

SERVES 8

- 4 egg whites
- 225g (8oz) caster sugar
- 2 teaspoons cornflour
- 2 teaspoons white wine vinegar
- 50g (2oz) shelled and roasted hazelnuts, roughly chopped

FOR THE FILLING

- 150ml (5fl oz) double cream, lightly whipped
- 200g tub of Greek-style yoghurt
- 4 passion fruit
- 1 large ripe mango, peeled and cut into slices

FOR THE COULIS

- 4 good tablespoons lemon curd
- 2 passion fruits

Lay a sheet of non-stick baking parchment on a large flat baking tray and mark with a 23cm (9 inch) circle. Preheat the oven to 160°C/140°C fan/gas 3.

Whisk the egg whites with an electric whisk on full speed, until stiff and looking like cloud. Add the sugar, a teaspoonful at a time, still whisking at full speed until it has all been incorporated. Blend the cornflour and white wine vinegar together in a small bowl and fold into the meringue mixture with the hazelnuts.

Spoon the mixture into the circle marked on the baking parchment on the baking tray and spread out gently so that the meringue forms a 23cm (9 inch) circle, building the sides up well so that they are higher than the middle.

Place in the preheated oven but immediately reduce the temperature setting to 150°C/130°C fan/gas 2. Bake the pavlova for about 1–1 1/2 hours, until firm to the touch and a pale beige in colour. Turn off the oven and allow the pavlova to become quite cold in the oven.

Carefully remove the pavlova from the baking tray, peel off the baking parchment and slide the pavlova on to a flat serving plate.

● ***The pavlova can be made up to a week ahead and kept wrapped in a cool place. Unfilled pavlova freezes well.***

Prepare the filling: mix the whipped cream and yoghurt together in a bowl. Cut the passion fruit in half and scoop out the seeds and juice. Stir together with the mango slices. Mix half the fruit with the cream and yoghurt.

Spoon into the centre of the pavlova, decorate with the remaining mango and passion fruit mixture. Leave in the fridge for about 1 hour before serving.

To make the coulis, mix the lemon curd with the scooped-out seeds and juice from the passion fruit, and serve with the pavlova.

AGA COOKING Bake in the simmering oven for about 2 hours until the pavlova is firm and easily comes off the baking parchment. If still a little sticky, sit on a tea towel on the lid of the simmering plate to dry out for about 30 minutes.

Nothing is nicer than a crumble after Sunday lunch on a winter's day. This one is very quick as no pre-cooking of the fruit is required. The blackberries could be frozen – if so, do not defrost them before adding them to the apples. Serve the crumble with cream or crème fraîche.

APPLE and blackberry crumble

SERVES 6

675g ($1\frac{1}{2}$lb) cooking apples, peeled
450g (1 lb) blackberries
100g (4oz) caster sugar
cream, to serve

FOR THE CRUMBLE TOPPING

175g (6oz) flour
75g (3oz) butter
75g (3oz) demerara sugar

Preheat the oven to 180°C/160°C fan/gas 4. You will need a deep ovenproof 1.8litre (3 pint) dish.

Core and slice the apples and put in the ovenproof dish. Scatter the blackberries over the top. Then sprinkle over the sugar and 3 tablespoons of water.

Make the topping by whizzing the flour, butter and sugar in a food processor (or rub them together by hand) until the mixture has the texture of breadcrumbs. Sprinkle this into the dish over the fruit. Pat down a little until even on top.

Cook in the preheated oven for about 45 minutes–1 hour, until the topping is golden brown and the fruit is tender. Serve hot with cream.

● ***Make completely up to 2 days ahead and keep covered in the fridge. Reheat, uncovered, in a hot oven to serve.***

AGA COOKING Bake on the grid shelf on the floor of the roasting oven, with the cold shelf on the second set of runners for 25–30 minutes, until topping is pale golden at the edges. Transfer the cold shelf to the centre of the simmering oven and sit the half-cooked crumble on top. Continue to cook in the simmering oven for a further 20 minutes, until the fruit is tender.

home *baking*

This unusual bread has a wonderful colour and texture. Fast-action dried yeast is easy to use and added with all the other ingredients. The rising of the dough can be done in an airing cupboard, on top of a boiler or just in a warm kitchen. In a cool kitchen it'll take longer. Peppadew peppers are small sweet peppers from South Africa bought in jars.

rosemary sweet POTATO bread

SERVES 12

450g (1 lb) sweet potatoes, peeled and cut into 2cm (1-inch) cubes
good knob of butter, plus more for the bowl and baking sheet
500g (1 lb 2 oz) strong white flour
7g packet of fast-action yeast
4 tablespoons olive oil
1 tablespoon salt
150ml (1/4 pint) lukewarm milk
50g (2 oz) mild Peppadew peppers, finely chopped
2 large sprigs of rosemary, 1 finely chopped
1 egg, beaten

Cook the sweet potato in salted water until tender. Drain and mash with the butter until smooth. Set aside to cool.

Put the flour, mashed sweet potato, yeast, oil, salt and milk together in the bowl of an electric mixer. Mix, using a dough hook, for about 4–5 minutes, until the dough has come together and has a smooth texture. If using a food processor, whiz until comes together and then knead by hand until it has a smooth texture.

Tip into a buttered glass bowl, cover with cling film and put in a warm place to rise until doubled in size.

Tip the dough on to a floured surface and knock back to its original shape with your hands. Add the Peppadew peppers and the chopped rosemary, and knead into the dough. Make a hole in the middle and shape the dough into a large doughnut ring shape. Sit it on a buttered baking sheet, cover with a large clean plastic bag and leave to prove in warm place for about 30 minutes, or until doubled in size again.

Preheat the oven to 220°C/200°fan/gas 7.

Glaze the bread with egg wash, then snip the rosemary sprig into little pieces and push these into the top of the dough.

Bake in the preheated oven for about 30 minutes until golden brown and when tapped on the bottom it should sound hollow.

● ***This can be made up to 48 hours ahead and kept wrapped in a cool place. It can be frozen for up to a month.***

AGA COOKING Rise and prove the dough on the back of the Aga. Bake on the grid shelf on the floor of the roasting oven for about 10 minutes then slide directly on to the floor of the oven for about 10 minutes, and the cold sheet on the second set of runners if too brown.

I'm sometimes asked for exactly this – no fat, no sugar and no dairy, and it's still delicious, as it is packed with dried fruit and has a wonderful moist texture. Do not line the loaf tin with paper as the cake will stick to it, just grease with butter.

dairy-free FRUIT cake

CUTS into 6–8 slices

butter for the tin
100g (4oz) dried stoned prunes, roughly chopped
150ml (1/4 pint) boiling water
75g (3oz) self-raising flour
1/2 teaspoon baking powder
1/2 teaspoon ground cinnamon
25g (1oz) ground almonds
250g (9oz) mixed dried fruit, such as apricots, plums, pears, peaches, apple, chopped into large pieces
3 tablespoons orange juice (from a carton)
3 tablespoons Demerara sugar

Preheat the oven to 180°C/160°C fan/gas 4 and generously butter a 500g (1 lb) loaf tin.

Measure the prunes into a heatproof bowl, pour over the boiling water and set aside to cool and plump up.

Measure the remaining ingredients except the Demerara sugar into a mixing bowl, stir until smooth and fold in prunes and their soaking water.

Spoon the thick paste into the tin, level the top and sprinkle with the Demerara sugar.

Bake in the preheated oven for about 50–60 minutes, until golden-brown and when tested with a skewer, the skewer comes out clean.

● *This can be made and kept wrapped in foil in fridge for up to a week. It also freezes well.*

AGA COOKING Slide on to the grid shelf on the floor of the roasting oven, with the cold shelf on the second set of runners, for about 30–35 minutes until golden brown.

This moist fatless tea bread goes such a long way when sliced and buttered we serve it for teas on garden open-days. Be warned, the uncooked mixture is really very thick.

builders' TEA bread

CUTS into about 20 slices

butter for the tin
450g (1 lb) mixed dried fruit e.g. raisins, sultanas, currants
1 regular tea bag soaked in 300 ml (1/2 pint) boiling water
2 eggs
450g (1 lb) self-raising flour
255g (8 oz) light muscovado sugar
demerara sugar

Preheat the oven to 180°C/160°C fan/gas 4. Butter and line a 23 x 28cm (9 x 12-inch) traybake tin or roasting tin.

Measure the fruit into a mixing bowl and pour over the tea, leave for few hours or overnight if possible, until nearly all the liquid is absorbed.

Break the eggs into a mixing bowl, add the flour and muscovado sugar and beat in. Stir in the soaked fruit and any unabsorbed liquid.

Spoon into the tin and spread out evenly. Sprinkle with the demerara sugar.

Bake for about an hour, or until firm in the centre and dark golden brown and shrinking from the sides of the tin. Turn out and allow to cool.

● *The tea bread can be made and kept wrapped in foil in an airtight container for up to 3 days. It also freezes well.*

Serve cut into very thin slices and well buttered. (The tea bread cuts into about 20 thin slices, butter and cut in half again giving 2 slices each for 20.)

AGA COOKING 2-oven: Bake on the lowest set of runners in the roasting oven with the cold sheet on the second set of runners for about 35 minutes, until dark golden brown and shrinking away from the sides. 3- and 4-oven: Bake on the lowest set of runners in the baking oven for about 35 minutes; if getting too brown, slide the cold sheet on second set of runners.

This German Christmas bread needs to be proved in a warm place – an airing cupboard is ideal or, if you have an Aga, sit the baking sheet on a tea towel and put on top of the simmering oven lid or on a 4-oven Aga on the side warming plate.

stollen

SERVES 10

225g (8oz) strong white flour
1/2 (7g) packet of fast-action yeast
50g (2oz) caster sugar
75g (3oz) very soft butter
1/2 teaspoon grated nutmeg
1 egg
5 tablespoons milk
grated zest of 1/2 lemon
175g (6oz) mixed dried fruit, such as raisins, currants, sultanas
100g (4oz) marzipan
icing sugar

Measure the first seven ingredients into a bowl and mix by hand or in a free-standing mixer, using a dough hook, until the dough comes together. Knead by hand on a floured work surface for 10 minutes or in a mixer for 5 minutes on a low speed, until the dough is soft, smooth, shiny and still slightly wet.

Put the dough into a lightly oiled bowl, cover with cling film and leave to rise in warm place for 1 1/2–2 hours or until it has doubled in size and is light and puffy.

Knock back the dough by hand or in the mixer, then knead in the lemon zest and fruit until they are evenly distributed. Roll the dough directly on to non-stick parchment to a 30 x 17cm (12 x 7inch) rectangle.

Roll the marzipan to a long sausage the same length as the dough. Lay this on the long side nearest to you and roll up like a Swiss roll. Seal the edges with the rolling pin and mould into a crescent with the sealed edge on the bottom. Slide the paper and stollen on to a baking sheet, cover with cling film or a large poly bag and tie the ends to create a warm atmosphere. Leave to prove in a warm place for the second rising for about 30–45 minutes or until it has doubled in size again. Preheat the oven to 190°C/170°fan/gas 5.

Remove the bag or cling film and bake in the oven for about 20–25 minutes, until light golden brown and the stollen sounds hollow when tapped underneath (check after 15 minutes, you may need to cover with foil if the top is getting too brown). Leave to cool, then dust heavily with icing sugar.

● *It will keep for up to a week in an airtight container in the fridge and it freezes well.*

After the first day, I serve Stollen warm like croissants. Slice off the amount you want in one piece, wrap loosely with foil and reheat in a moderate oven for 15 minutes or wrap in cling film and microwave. Slice thickly to serve.

AGA COOKING Bake on the grid shelf on the floor of the roasting oven, with the cold sheet on the second set of runners for 10–15 minutes, then turn the stollen around and change the cold sheet. Bake for another 10–15 minutes, until golden brown and sounding hollow when tapped underneath.

These are breakfast-style muffins. If you have difficulty getting buttermilk, use low-fat plain yoghurt or milk instead.

fresh RASPBERRY and almond muffins

MAKES 12

325g (11oz) self-raising flour
225g (8oz) caster sugar
1 teaspoon baking powder
50g (2oz) blanched chopped almonds
2 eggs
100g (4oz) butter, melted, plus more for the tin (optional)
284ml carton of buttermilk
1/2 teaspoon almond extract
150g (5oz) fresh raspberries

Preheat the oven to 200°C/180°C fan/gas 6. Butter a 12-hole deep muffin tin or line it with paper muffin cases.

Mix together the flour, sugar, baking powder and two-thirds of the almonds in a bowl.

In a separate bowl, mix together the eggs, the 100g (4oz) melted butter, buttermilk and almond extract, and whisk until blended.

Pour the liquid on to the flour mixture and mix until smooth (being careful not to overbeat). Stir in the raspberries.

Spoon into the prepared muffin tin, sprinkle with the remaining almonds and bake in the preheated oven for about 20–25 minutes, until risen, golden brown and shrinking away from the sides of the tins.

● ***These can be made up to 3 days ahead, then refreshed in a moderate oven for about 10 minutes to serve. They also freeze well.***

AGA COOKING Slide on to the grid shelf on the floor of the roasting oven, with the cold shelf on the second set of runners, for about 20 minutes, until well risen, golden brown and shrinking away from the sides of the tin.

These thick pieces of shortbread have a wonderful subtle ginger flavour, with real ginger pieces in the shortbread. For a change, add a little grated zest of 1 small orange.

GINGER spiced shortbread

MAKES 18 biscuits

100g (4oz) softened butter, plus more for the tin
50g (2oz) light muscovado sugar
100g (4oz) plain flour
50g (2oz) cornflour
1 level teaspoon ground ginger
50g (2oz) stem ginger, chopped into raisin-sized pieces
demerara sugar, for sprinkling

Preheat the oven to 180°C/160°C fan/gas 4. Butter a shallow 18cm (7-inch) square tin.

Measure the butter and muscovado sugar together in a bowl and beat until smooth.

Add the remaining ingredients except the Demerara sugar and bring together with your hands to form a dough. Tip into the prepared tin and press with back of a spoon to even out. Prick all over with a fork and sprinkle with a little Demerara sugar.

Bake in the preheated oven for about 25–30 minutes, until pale golden-brown and firm. While still warm, cut 3 equal lines each way to produce 9 squares and then cut each square diagonally into triangles.

● ***Store these in a plastic storage box or cake tin for up to a week. They also freeze well.***

AGA COOKING Bake on the grid shelf on the floor of the roasting oven, with the cold sheet on the second set of runners, for about 15 minutes until pale golden, then transfer to the simmering oven for a further 20 minutes to cook through.

These are seriously good – perfect for coffee mornings, picnics or special occasions.

CHOCOLATE raisin cookies

MAKES 18

100g (4oz) butter, softened, plus more for the baking sheets
50g (2oz) caster sugar
100g (4oz) self-raising flour
25g (1oz) cocoa powder
75g (3oz) packet of chocolate-coated raisins

Preheat the oven to 180°C/160°C fan/gas 4 and butter 2 baking sheets.

Cream the butter and sugar together in a bowl until soft and fluffy.

Add the flour and cocoa, and mix for a few moments until a dough ball forms. Knead in the raisins.

Shape into 18 small round balls and arrange on the prepared baking sheets, giving room between them to allow them to spread a little). Press the balls down with a fork.

Bake in the preheated oven for about 10–12 minutes, until nearly firm and mahogany-brown. Leave to cool on the tray, then transfer to a wire rack.

● ***These can be stored in an airtight container for up to a week. They also freeze well.***

AGA COOKING Bake on the grid shelf on the floor of the roasting oven, with the cold sheet on the second set of runners, for about 10 minutes, or until nearly firm and mahogany-brown; leave to cool on the tray, then transfer to a wire rack.

This is quite the best chocolate cake around. Make in a traybake tin, as here, or in two 20cm (8-inch) sandwich tins.

chocolate TRAYBAKE *with ganache icing*

CUTS into 24 pieces

100g (4oz) butter, softened, plus more for the tin
50g (2oz) cocoa powder
6 tablespoons boiling water
3 eggs
4 tablespoons milk
175g (6oz) self-raising flour
1 rounded teaspoon baking powder
300g (10oz) caster sugar

FOR THE GANACHE ICING

150g (5oz) Bournville chocolate or similar
150ml (5fl oz) double cream
3 tablespoons apricot jam, warmed

Preheat the oven to 180°C/160°fan/gas 5. Butter and line a traybake tin or small roasting tin with foil about 30 x 23cm (12 x 9 inches).

Sieve the cocoa powder into a bowl. Add the boiling water and mix together to a smooth paste. Add the 100g (4oz) butter, the eggs, milk, flour, baking powder and sugar, and mix together using a hand mixer. Turn into the lined traybake tin and level the top.

Bake in the oven for about 20–25 minutes, until well risen and shrinking away from the edges. Leave to cool while making the icing.

● ***The cake can be made and iced up to 48 hours ahead and kept in the fridge. The cake freezes well iced or un-iced; we prefer to freeze un-iced and then ice fresh on the day.***

To make the icing: in a bowl over a pan of just-simmering water, melt the chocolate in the double cream until smooth and runny. Stir and leave to cool and thicken up to an icing consistency.

Spread the jam over the cake, then spread over the icing and smooth with a palette knife. Cut into pieces to serve.

AGA COOKING Bake on the grid shelf on the floor of the roasting oven with the cold sheet on the second set of runners for about 30–35 minutes, until shrinking away from the sides of the tin and springy to the touch.

This is a really deep luxurious coffee cake – very impressive and delicious. If you are worried about cutting the cakes in half, you can just sandwich the two together with half the icing in the middle and half the icing on top.

cappuccino coffee cake

SERVES 8

225g (8oz) very soft butter, plus more for the tins
225g (8oz) light muscovado sugar or caster sugar
225g (8oz) self-raising flour
1 teaspoon baking powder
4 large eggs
4 level teaspoons instant coffee, dissolved in 1 tablespoon boiling water

FOR THE COFFEE ICING

175g (6oz) soft butter
350g (12oz) icing sugar
4 level teaspoons instant coffee, dissolved in 1 tablespoon boiling water

Preheat the oven to 180°C/160°C fan/gas 4. Butter and line the base of two deep 20cm (8 inch) sandwich cake tins.

Measure all the cake ingredients, except the coffee, into a large mixing bowl and beat together until smooth. Stir in the dissolved mixture until thoroughly blended. Divide the mixture evenly between the 2 prepared tins and level the tops.

Bake in the preheated oven for about 25–30 minutes until golden brown, shrinking away from the sides of the tin and the sponge springs back when lightly pressed.

To make the icing, mix the butter and sugar together in a mixing bowl and beat together until smooth. Beat in the dissolved coffee and divide into 4. When the cakes are cold, slice each cake horizontally in half giving 4 layers of cake. Sit one base on a cake stand and spread with a quarter of the mixture. Continue layering up with cake and icing so you finish with icing on top and swirl to give an attractive finish.

● ***The cake can be made and iced up to 2 days ahead, kept covered in the fridge. Iced or un-iced, the cake freezes well.***

AGA COOKING 2-oven Aga: Bake on the grid shelf on the floor of the roasting oven, with the cold sheet on the second set of runners, for about 25 minutes until golden brown. 3- and 4-oven Aga: Bake on the grid shelf on the floor of the baking oven for about 25 minutes. If getting too brown, slide the cold sheet on the second set of runners.

This simple banana sponge will be very popular as it is fairly deep but has a crunchy lemon topping.

banana with lemon DRIZZLE cake

SERVES 6–8

175g (6oz) butter, softened, plus more for the tin
175g (6oz) caster sugar
3 eggs
300g (10oz) self-raising flour
2 level teaspoons baking powder
2 ripe bananas, peeled and mashed
grated zest of 1/2 lemon
2 tablespoons milk

FOR THE TOPPING

juice of 1 lemon
100g (4oz) granulated sugar

Preheat the oven to 180°C/160°C fan/gas 5. Line the base of a 20cm (8inch) deep round cake tin and butter the sides.

Measure the cake ingredients into a large mixing bowl. Mix together until smooth, using a hand-mixer or beat by hand. Pour into the lined tin and level the top.

Bake in the preheated oven for about 45–50 minutes, until light golden brown. Test with a skewer to see if the cake is cooked through; if the skewer comes out clean, the cake is cooked. Leave to cool down a little, then remove from the tin.

Make the topping by mixing together the ingredients in a bowl. Pour over the warm cake and spread out to the edges. Leave to become completely cold before slicing.

● **The cake can be made and iced up to 48 hours ahead and kept in a dry sealed container. It also freezes well, iced or un-iced.**

AGA COOKING 2-, 3- and 4-oven: Bake on the grid shelf on the floor of the roasting oven, with the cold sheet on the second set of runners, for 30 minutes, until light brown. Transfer the hot cold sheet to the simmering oven, put the cake on top and cook for a further 25 minutes until, set.

It has been a sheer pleasure to write this book with the same wonderful supportive team as usual. Lucy Young (near left) came straight from Cordon Bleu college – shy, keen and so willing to learn – and now she runs the show! Although still helping me, she is now also an author in her own right, with three books published, the latest being Secrets of Aga Cakes. Luc and I are a team, and I hope will be together for many years to come. All the recipes are tried and tested just as many times as it takes to get them right. This is the daily task of Lucinda Kaizik (far left), the third member of our team, and there are always shoals of family and friends to taste what is cooked. We have great fun in doing all this and I thank both Lucy and Lucinda greatly.

The Quadrille team were also so enthusiastic from day one and have worked with us constantly to produce the best possible book. Our thanks to Editorial Director, Jane O'Shea, and our editor Lewis Esson, who was just the best. I was simply delighted by the look of the book and the photography – no fashionable dreamy out-of-focus shots, just beautiful clear food. Thanks for this are due to Art Director Mary Evans, photographer Martin Brigdale, prop stylist Helen Trent and food stylist Annie Rigg.